The Ethics of Caring

The Ethics of Caring

Honoring the Web of Life in Our Professional Healing Relationships

Kylea Taylor

Hanford Mead Publishers

Santa Cruz, California

Grateful acknowledgment is made for permission to reprint excerpts from the following works: From IMAGERY IN HEALING by Jeanne Achterberg © 1985. Printed by arrangement with Shambhala Publications, Inc., 300 Massachusetts Avenue, Boston, MA 02115. From BEYOND THE BRAIN by Stanislav Grof © 1985 by permission of State University of New York Press. From POWER IN THE HELPING PROFESSIONS by Adolf Guggenbühl-Craig © 1971 by permission of Spring Publications, Inc., 299 E. Quassett Rd, Woodstock, CT 06281. From THE FAMILY THERAPY NETWORKER, 7705 Thirteenth Street NW, Washington, DC 20012. From SOMATICS, Somatic Novato Institute for Somatic Research and Training, 1576 Grant Ave # 220, Novato, CA 94945. From ETHICS IN PSYCHOTHERAPY by K. S. Pope & M. J. T. Vasquez, © 1991 by permission of Jossey Bass, Inc., Publishers. From "Sexual Involvement Between Therapists and Patients" by K. S. Pope © 1994 by permission of the Harvard Medical School Health Publications Group. From "On Defining Spirit" by Rachel Naomi Remen © 1988. From THE SHAMAN'S BODY by Arnold Mindell © 1993 by permission of HarperCollins Publishers. From SPEAKING FROM THE HEART by Rita C. Manning © 1992 by permission of Rowman & Littlefield Publishers, Inc. From "What do women want? by Pythia Peay © 1994.

Permission to quote from their ethical codes and guidelines was granted by American Association for Marriage and Family Therapy, American Association of Professional Hypnotherapists, American Group Psychotherapy Association, Inc., American Psychiatric Association, American Psychological Association, The Australian N.S.W., Victorian, and Queensland Emotional Release Counsellors Associations, False Memory Syndrome Foundation, Jin Shin Do® Foundation, and National Association for Music Therapy, Inc.

SECOND EDITION

ISBN No. 0-9643158-1-5 (alk. paper)

Manufactured in the United States of America

8 7 6 5

This edition is printed on acid-free paper that meets the American National Standards Institute Z39.48 Standard.

To all my teachers

Acknowledgments

I would like to acknowledge some people who helped shape *The Ethics of Caring*. My professor of ethics in a traditional graduate school allowed me to choose a radical topic for a paper. That paper grew into this book.

Christina Grof was the first and strongest voice to validate that the perspective on ethics in this book was worth pursuing. I appreciate her encouragement and ideas. Stanislav Grof continues to show me how to trust the process, both in myself and in those with whom I work. I am deeply grateful to them both for designing Holotropic Breathwork™ and providing a model for the ethical exploration of profound states of consciousness.

Over the past seven years at the East/West Retreats, Jack Kornfield has inspired me with his example as a leader and as a human being. Observing him as he is present with people, I have realized how each moment of ethical motivation and action on the part of a caregiver can support right relationship and healing. I am so honored that he has written the *Foreword* for this book.

Many people contributed suggestions and additions to *The Ethics of Caring*. I am thankful to those who gave a significant amount of their time to read and suggest improvements to the manuscript in its various stages. Hal Zina Bennett encouraged me at a particularly low point. He proposed the present title of the book as a vast improvement over the one I was considering, and I was able to jump back into production. Christina Grof and Jack Kornfield also made very practical editing suggestions that changed the tone and the craftsmanship of the manuscript.

Alia Moore, my dear friend for twenty-five years, was the first person to whom I dared show a few chapters. Her suggestions kept me going and influenced the model quite a bit. I appreciate also Katherine Ziegler's editing and discussion of ethical concepts, our peer supervision together, and the work we have done to begin teaching a new perspective on ethics. I thank Robert R. Newport for reading the manuscript and writing many helpful comments and examples. His viewpoint from both medical and spiritual studies added breadth to the book.

My thanks also to graphic designer Daniel Cook who was able to take a difficult abstract theme like ethics and turn it into a beautiful, abstract "honoring the web of life" cover design.

I also want to acknowledge Sunflower House, a Therapeutic Community in Santa Cruz, which both teaches and practices ethical caring in community. I owe Sunflower House a great deal.

I am especially grateful to my daughter, Taylor Albright, and my partner, Jim Schofield. Without their extensive copyediting, their ever ready wise advice in production matters, and general loving support this book could not have been published.

Contents

Chapter 6—   89

Sex

Chapter 7—   105

Power

Chapter 8—   119

Love

oreword

The Ethics of Caring is an extraordinarily helpful and groundbreaking new book for healers, clergy, therapists, and bodyworkers that illuminates what is necessary to offer wise and trustworthy relations to their clients. It teaches in detail and example the ways to understand and deepen the beauty of one's integrity as a healing professional. Traditionally this study is called *ethics*, but to expand the moralistic and sin-like tone ethics has often taken on, Kylea has grounded her work in the spiritual principle of *reverence for life* that underlies all the world's great religions and healing systems.

In this Kylea has contributed many new dimensions of ethics, first by carefully articulating a very wide range of traditional concerns in areas such as truthfulness, confidentiality, informed consent and clear sexual boundaries. Then with equal clarity she elaborates upon the basic principles of non-harming as they are needed for the vast terrain of healing realms, including crisis of trauma, loss and grief work, spiritual counseling, expanded consciousness, energetic and shamanic openings, and much more.

In exploring this greatly broadened territory, *The Ethics of Caring* alerts healers not to underestimate the power of energies that arise in nonordinary states through transference and countertransference, and the palpable physical, emotional, and psychic vulnerabilities that come in these states. To help readers understand this terrain, Kylea illustrates what particular difficulties may arise in relation to each of the basic human energy centers or chakras, offering keys to understand how healers may be caught by these energies. She demonstrates through example and exercises how the fears and needs of the healers, sexually, financially, emotionally, and spiritually can become entangled with their clients, especially with the heightened sensitivity and suggestibility found in regressed and transpersonal dimensions.

To read and take to heart this book requires a great degree of truthfulness on the part of the reader. To reflect on *The Ethics of Caring* is healing and therapeutic in itself, as it brings our consciousness to the potential shadow areas of all healing relationships. Through the exercises provided, and by thoughtful consideration, a healer can use this book to awaken a whole new level of awareness in the areas which have the greatest potential to bring conflict and harm.

And indeed, this is Kylea's greatest gift and offering. From her own years of inner experience and deep exploration, she illuminates these areas for us. She wisely insists that every minister, healer, therapist, bodyworker, and shaman who ventures into the vast territory of the psyche can only offer the light of consciousness that they have encountered and made their own. Their own grief and personal history, their true passion and spiritual nature, their understanding of the difficult task of opening in themselves is their gift. This is the fundamental prerequisite for a true healer, together with the ethics and virtue that Kylea articulates so well.

My own Buddhist Master Achaan Chah loved to talk about this virtue of non-harming, calling it the ground of all true spiritual life. Kylea has honored this ground of healing with her work. Especially in our modern times, where the necessity of integrity for the human heart has been lost in the speed, complexity and ambition that drives consumer society, we need voices of care and respect that Kylea represents. This is the basis for true healing.

For this I offer Kylea my gratitude and congratulations. May her work bring protection, understanding and compassionate blessings to all who guide and heal.

Jack Kornfield, Ph.D.
Spirit Rock Center
Woodacre, California
1995

 **reface**

W hile studying to obtain my master's degree in marriage and family counseling, I was required to take a course in ethics. Although touching on philosophical issues, this course was more like a law course than a counseling course. Because of state licensing requirements, the professor's emphasis was on teaching us how to avoid litigation rather than on encouraging us to examine our own values, motivations, and relationships with our clients.

In talking with others who have studied in related fields, be it psychology, other healing arts, or the ministry, I have found that this same approach to ethics education prevails. Yet I have come to believe that a close examination of ethical issues and of our personal relationship to them could be more than merely learning a set of rules and finding ways to protect ourselves from the perils of legal prosecution. I believe that such an examination can give us precious insights into ourselves and our sacred relationships with our clients—insights which may be as deep as those we receive from any other part of our training or education.

One of the most important concepts of the caring professions in modern times is the idea that the caregiver herself and what she brings to the caring situation as a person is more important to the outcome of the care than the choice of technique she employs in giving the care. The caregiver must have the ability to travel deeply and empathetically with the client into uncharted and often frightening territory. In order to navigate effectively, the caregiver must have familiarity with the territory, understanding of the difficulties and the pain that may be encountered, and most of all a sense of trust that it is indeed safe and ultimately healing to travel through these areas. Professional training which incorporates emphasis on self-examination and inner exploration could enable caregivers to gain the familiarity and confidence in these explorations which are necessary to hold the light for others.

I believe that the study of ethical issues can provide insights which are invaluable to the caregiver in understanding the client's psychological process, as well as her own. These issues surround the most difficult, sensitive, and potentially most dangerous aspects of the client-caregiver relationship. Ethical issues pertain to longings, feelings, and motivations which resonate at our very core. Our drives toward (and away from) money, sexuality, power, love, truth, inspiration, and oneness are the most powerful forces in our lives. How can we expect that these drives will not intrude in one way or another into our relationships with clients? Only by understanding these aspects of ourselves and by deeply considering the ways in which they affect our interactions with others can we hope to enter more fully into truly healing relationships with our clients.

The Ethics of Caring attempts to provide some navigational tools for dealing with the deep and often confusing interaction between client and caregiver. It particularly addresses those instances where we as caregivers spontaneously encounter, or help to induce through specific techniques, intense and profound experiences in our clients. These extraordinary shared experiences in the context of the therapeutic relationship can bring to the surface compelling fears, needs, and longings in both the client and the caregiver.

Others have called the states of consciousness in which these intense experiences arise by various names: therapeutic breakthroughs, abreaction, regression, altered states, shamanic states, ecstatic states, and peak experiences. I have chosen to use the broad term *nonordinary states of consciousness* to include any state of consciousness in which there is heightened sensitivity and awareness and in which there can arise a variety of specific phenomena not usually recognized by traditional psychology (See *Chapter 2*). I hope my model, which does recognize spiritual longings and the psychospiritual phenomena of an expanded therapeutic paradigm, will widen our range of ethical choices as professionals, narrow the scope of ignorance, and support the delicate, individual process of ethical development.

In *The Ethics of Caring*, I present the consideration of ethics from this new perspective. I have drawn examples from my own experience and that of others who have so generously told me their stories. These include both clients and caregivers alike, who have wounded or been wounded in some way because of the powerful forces involved. Also, I have drawn examples, where possible, from what literature is available on the subject and have tried to be careful to give credit when such is the case. I hope you will join me on an interesting journey to explore how our lives are touched by ethical issues and will share with me some of the excitement I feel when examining these provocative questions.

1

An Ethic of Relationship

An ethic of care involves a morality grounded in relationship and response.[1]

—Rita C. Manning

Ethics has to do with the most interesting parts of human life: sex, relationship, self-understanding, love, and mysticism. Ethics, like sex (which it often seems to concern), is arousing, engaging, and often amusing. The consideration of ethics has the potential to expand self-knowledge and self-concept, and to improve relationships.

Ethics concerns relationship. It is about the inner relationships of our values to actions. It is interaction between one belief and another, one desire and another, one fear and another. Ethics is the process by which we sort out what best creates inner and outer harmony in our lives.

Honoring the web of life

Ethical behavior stems from the *internal* congruency and harmony between our values and our actions. Ethical behavior also develops from the caregiver's sense of *external* connection. Using nonordinary states of consciousness, the caregiver works with not only all parts of a client, but all parts of the network to which the client is connected (or from which she has become disconnected). She works with those parts physically, emotionally, cognitively, socially, and existentially or spiritually. Emotional, physical, and spiritual healing takes into account the sociopolitical system (and perhaps even the cosmological system) within which the therapeutic relationship itself exists. We speak more ethically and act more ethically when we begin to see and honor the web-like context of relationship that weaves among the many facets of both caregiver and client. We naturally make more ethical decisions when we honor the intricate connections extending beyond the walls of the therapy session into family, culture, ecosystem, and even into unseen dimensions.

An ethic of relationship must address the web of relationship that extends beyond immediate personal relationships to people of other races and nations and to all living things. Czech Republic President Vaclav Havel (1994) spoke of what he called the "forgotten dimension of democracy . . . that spiritual dimension that connects all cultures and in fact all humanity." He spoke about the ethics of politics being an ability to see the commonality in humanity, and said that, "many politicians or regimes espouse these ideas in words but do not apply them in practice."[2]

Havel's message was that transcendence—a spiritual perspective beyond personal, ethnic, religious, or chauvinistic viewpoints—would result in ethical relationship on a global scale. He said that loss of respect for our transcendental origins "always leads to loss of respect for everything else—from the laws people have made for themselves, to the life of their neighbours and of our living planet."[3]

The principle of interconnection that Havel expresses is what I am calling the *web of life*. The web of life metaphor describes the interconnectedness, not only of sociopolitical systems and ethnic groups, but interconnectedness between individuals demonstrated in many ways, from their financial relationships and conversations to their dreams. The web of life is demonstrated also by the mysterious phenomena of synchronicity, by the power of prayer and shamanic healing mechanisms, and by the capacity of love and positive regard of one person to be therapeutic to another. *What I do affects you. What you do affects me. What I do to you will ultimately affect me.*

What is ethics?

Ethics is the study of morality. The study of morals in the therapeutic relationship involves reflection upon the ideals we aspire to as caregivers and contemplation of our actual behavior. Rachel Naomi Remen in her article *On Defining Spirit* says that "ethics is a set of values, a code for translating the moral into daily life."[4] In both morality and self-reflection about our own ethics we engage with our own (sometimes unconscious) inner dialogue between our values and our actions. When we examine ethical issues which pertain particularly to work with clients in nonordinary states, we delve into material that can be even more subtle and interesting than the ethical issues that arise in the course of our ordinary interactions with clients.

Considering ethical issues helps us move along on our own psychospiritual journeys without taking detours. When we avoid taking detours, we are more present with ourselves and our clients and can more easily follow the first rule of therapeutic work, *do no harm.*

Moving toward wholeness

We judge the ethics of a caregiver by her behavior. We think of highly ethical behavior as having integrity. Another word for integrity is wholeness. Wholeness means that a caregiver's behavior is congruent with her values, knowledge, intuition, and feelings. Integrity means that there is harmonious, consensual dialogue between different internal functions which results in external behavior that is consistent and ethical.

Integrity can also mean that ethical behavior, which because of human nature always falls short of perfection, is at least behavior which is moving towards wholeness or integrity. Stanislav and Christina Grof, developers of Holotropic Breathwork™, coined the word *holotropic* to describe therapeutic work in nonordinary states which assists a client in moving toward mental, physical, psychological, and spiritual wholeness. This word *holotropic* could also be used to describe the process of therapists, teachers, and caregivers moving toward wholeness—expanding their ethical consciousness to include more and more integrity: *holotropic ethics*. Such an understanding of ethics goes beyond morals and ethical codes. Rather, morality and ethical behavior are in the service of our highest nature and are at the same time a natural product of our growing attunement with our spiritual natures. Rachel Naomi Remen distinguishes *moral* from *spiritual*:

> *What is considered moral varies from culture to culture and from time to time within the same culture. Furthermore, morality often serves as the basis for judgment, for one group of people separating themselves from other groups, or one individual separating from others. Yet the spiritual is profoundly nonjudgmental and non-separative. The spiritual does not vary from time to time because it is not within time. Spirit is unchanging.*[5]

Ethics goes beyond law and guidelines

My graduate school psychology ethics textbook said that the purpose of studying morals was, like law, "to outline rules of conduct that assist in harmonious living and the facilitation of achievement of individual aims and desires in a socially acceptable manner."[6] Professional ethical standards usually reach far beyond the law and stipulate certain unprofessional conduct that, while legally allowed, is not ethically permissible.

Such standards specify those behaviors which have proven counter-therapeutic and are therefore considered unacceptable by the professional community. In other words, sets of ethical guidelines encourage behavior that is most effective therapeutically and discourage behavior that is ineffective or therapeutically harmful. When a code of ethics prohibits the professional from advancing her personal or business interests through her professional relationship with a client, this is an example of a code defining unethical, but not necessarily illegal, behavior.

Like the law, most of the ethical standards were originally written as rules applied because of abstract principles of right and wrong. If codes are too rigid, they may not even allow for justice to be done. The trend in ethical codes seems to be moving away from the format that mimics a legal code. Guidelines need to be flexible enough to enable an educational, rather than a punitive experience to occur. The language of some ethical codes is beginning to sound less legalistic and more as if written to promote awareness of motivation and agreement on values. Rather than legislating behavior in many cases, ethical codes are addressing these origins of ethical behavior. (See *Chapter 14.*)

Ethical decisions based on relationship rather than abstract principles

With the advent of feminism, research began to show that the model of abstract principles did not work as well for women as it did for men. Carol Gilligan, author of *In a Different Voice*, writes that women make decisions, especially ethical decisions, differently than men. According to her studies, women make such decisions, not by using abstract principles, but in the context of relationship.[7] For example, if someone steals food to feed another person, even if stealing remains illegal, do the circumstances make this an ethical act, rather than an unethical act?

The Ethics of Caring looks at ethics from the point of view of relationship rather than law. Rita Manning, who wrote *Speaking from the Heart: A Feminist Perspective on Ethics*, writes about an ethic of care. She differentiates this kind of ethical response from a more rigid moral pose in this way:

> *An ethic of care involves a morality grounded in relationship and response . . . . In responding, we do not appeal to abstract principles, though we may appeal to rules of thumb; rather we pay attention to the concrete other in his or her real situation. We also pay attention to the effect of our response on the networks of care that sustain us both.*[8]

Ethics in the context of profound work with clients

Working with clients who have intense moments in a therapeutic session or who have temporarily entered nonordinary states of consciousness can sometimes bring ethical challenges to caregivers. Certain intense and profound experiences in clients can produce subtle and powerful motivations in caregivers. These experiences tend to make boundaries more diffuse, confuse roles, intensify transference and trigger surprisingly compelling countertransference. Intense therapeutic work may present extraordinary ethical challenges. On the other hand, because these clients provide caregivers with choices between various ethical actions and present many gray areas with many levels of consequence to any action, they also offer enormous creative opportunity for personal and professional development.

The answers are not cut and dried. When is it ethical or unethical to touch a client, for example? Is the same behavior ethical at one time and unethical at another, depending on the circumstances and the motivations of a caregiver? When is "dual relationship" an appropriate and conscientious acknowledgment of human connection, and when is it problematic or exploitative?

To answer these questions, we can share information among ourselves, offer guidelines, make agreements, and get consultation. In many cases, however, we cannot determine the best choice of behavior without feeling and looking at all the implications of the particular action in a situation. Even then, our action, based on logical application of abstract principles to a specific situation, may be less ethical than a response which arises out of heartfelt caring in conjunction with self-examination of our own motivations.

What is ethical behavior?

If we do not stipulate conduct through rules and abstract principles, how then do we raise ethical standards in our professions? Guidelines are necessary, but relying on others to legislate what are *unethical* behaviors can help us maintain an external locus of control with regard to ethical decisions. Self-examination of values and motivations, on the other hand, stimulates the development of an internal locus of control for those professionals among us who sincerely want to expand our ethical consciousness.

Ethical *external* locus of control means that the caregiver is looking to external guidelines or someone else's rules to determine her own behavior. Ethical *internal* locus of control means that the caregiver may be reading about ethical guidelines, but ultimately, she is checking her own values and motivations to determine a course of action.

The lack of a developed internal locus of control with regard to ethics becomes exponentially more apparent when the caregiver is working with nonordinary states. Where we are "coming from"—our motivations and values as therapists and caregivers—is the source of what we do and say. The degree of our willingness to delve into the dark truth of our own motivations, desires, and fears will determine our ability to be caring, flexible, and ethical.

"Disconnection" in the context of connection

Ethical therapy nurtures the context of connection while allowing a client to take actions which seem to "disconnect" her from all these systems. That is, therapy and caregiving affirm a system of connection because the client chooses *relationship* itself as a vehicle for healing. A child who has disconnected from her family and her family's values by acting out has not really disconnected from the family system. In fact, family systems theory operates on the assumption that the child cares enough about the family to act out, even at the expense of punishment for her bad behavior. Many disconnected children are unconsciously hoping to draw the family together by giving the system a reason to come together to solve a problem. The child's disconnection or acting out often occurs in the context of relationship and caring.

The therapeutic relationship assumes client wholeness and the client's ability to integrate, while at the same time understanding and validating the client's choice (whether conscious or not) to dissociate at times during the process of surviving or healing. A caregiver with a transcendent viewpoint holds relationship, connection, and association as the more expanded version of truth than separation. She understands that the truth of relationship can contain the truth of disconnection.

The ethic of relationship also extends into nonordinary reality, particularly with regard to transpersonal (beyond the personal identity) experiences. Clients have relationships with God or Goddess, their Higher Power, power animals, spirit guides, or numinous forces that bring them healing and wisdom. When both the caregiver and client neither deny nor exploit, but rather acknowledge and honor these relationships which exist in nonordinary states of consciousness, their actions naturally become ethical.

Ethical development requires transcendence

If ethics is the study of relationship, then transcending the viewpoint that we are unrelated is requisite for ethical development. Transcendent viewpoint develops within one person at a time. It can happen simultaneously in groups, even large groups, but the transcendent experience is an internal one, not an external one. A commonly used metaphor for transcendence of the self through inner work is this one: *We all have to dive into our own well to reach the underground river that connects all sources of water.*

Therapy and other forms of caregiving are contexts for the growth of the transcendent cultural viewpoint through the transcendent individual experience. Spiritual fellowship and group rituals are others. These are all means by which we expand our ability to realize our relatedness. Therapy is one medium through which we can practice truly ethical behavior with each other. Therapy's influence on the web of life begins in the primary relationship between client and caregiver. Mary Sykes Wylie, writing about family therapy, muses that, "in some sense, the most perplexing aspect of therapy is that the relationship itself between therapist and client *is* the service delivered."[9] This can also be true for the relationships between bodyworker and client, clergyperson and congregation member, or hospice worker and dying patient.

My personal definition of ethical behavior borrows from the term *reverence for life* used by the Christian medical missionary philosopher, Albert Schweitzer. It also uses the concept of *right relationship* from Buddhism.

Schweitzer was famous for the philosophy he practiced in every detail of daily living called *reverence for life*. He describes what he meant in a sermon that he delivered in 1919: "I cannot but have reverence for all that is called life. . . . That is the beginning and foundation of morality. Once a man has experienced it and continues to do so—and he who has once experienced it will continue to do so—he is ethical. He carries his morality within him and can never lose it, for it continues to develop within him. He who has never experienced this has only a set of superficial principles. These theories have no root in him, they do not belong to him, and they fall off him."[10]

His *reverence for life* contains the implicit acknowledgment of relationship which he verbalized as he accepted the Nobel Prize for Peace in 1952: "You do not live in a world all alone. Your brothers are here too."[11]

The Buddhist concept of *right relationship* is akin to Jesus' injunction, *Do unto others as you would have them do unto you.*[12] It implies that we see the bigger picture of how our intention and actions in relationship affect the *other*, and how that in turn affects still others in a rippling outward motion. It implies that we see also the effects on ourselves when we take certain actions toward others. In this definition the concept of *others* applies to persons and animals, but also to plants, ecosystems, planets, and numinous archetypes.

Here then is my definition for ethical behavior which underlies what I have written in this book: *Ethical behavior is reverence for life demonstrated by right relationship to another.*

2

Profound and Intense Client Experiences

*An intellectual knowledge of the inner territories
. . . can be of great help to individuals experiencing
nonordinary states of consciousness,
whether planned and induced by known means or unsolicited and spontaneous.*

—Christina and Stanislav Grof

The ethical issues pertaining to caregiving become much more obvious when clients are having intense and profound experiences. It was in these kinds of circumstances that I first noticed the more subtle ethical issues. A piano teacher I knew used to say, *play loudly so you can hear your mistakes!* With both the client and the therapist *playing intensely,* we can learn lessons that we would not notice in those more quiet therapeutic situations. These lessons apply also to caregiving situations of ordinary intensity.

The concepts in this book took shape because of the amplification effect of intense sessions, but many of these ideas apply quite well to caregiving relationships which are neither as intense nor as profound. I have taken more effort in this chapter to describe the profound qualities of nonordinary states of consciousness and the characteristic experiences which often accompany them in clients. I have done this because the Western tradition of caregiving (medical, psycho-logical, and spiritual) is not usually very familiar with these by name and type.

I see in my work how this unfamiliarity, when intertwined with extremely powerful spiritual longings and energies, often experienced when working with clients in nonordinary states, can more readily compel caregivers to unconscious, unethical acts. Many caregivers, although they may be unfamiliar with the terminology, will recognize these characteristic experiences when I describe them. Therapists, ministers, and bodyworkers have undoubtedly encountered clients with some of the symptoms and issues which arise in nonordinary states.

What is a nonordinary state of consciousness?

I will start first by defining ordinary states. Ordinary states of consciousness are normal and usual for most people in Western cultures. We spend most of our time in these ordinary states: working, studying, calculating, talking, writing letters, playing games, cooking, diapering the baby, mowing the lawn, or driving the car. In an ordinary state of consciousness, we are usually busy interacting with the material world and other human beings who are also in ordinary states of consciousness. We are pretty clear about who we are. We know our name, address, social security number, and with whom we live. We know the other characteristics which define us, such as our gender, body type, age, education, and beliefs. Ordinary states of consciousness are important to our functioning in the world of matter.[13]

Nonordinary states of consciousness are less usual, but quite normal and important to our functioning as human beings. These states enable us to expand our sense of who we are. Clients in therapy, spiritual practitioners in meditation or religious ritual, or cli-

ents receiving a massage are often in nonordinary states of consciousness—mild to deep trance states in which their awareness is
focused in a different way than in ordinary life. The different
quality of awareness available in nonordinary states helps us increase our sense of connection to other people and to the world
around us and find meaning in our lives. Nonordinary states of
consciousness are important to our functioning in the very real, but
less tangible, world of emotion, energetic phenomena, intuition,
and spirit.[14]

We acknowledge nonordinary states less often in our Western
lives; nonetheless, these states are real, and everyone has experienced some state of nonordinary consciousness. Light trance states
occur normally in everyone throughout the day. Some examples of
more noticeable nonordinary states include: dreaming, lucid
dreaming, precognition, intense concentration, daydreaming,
childbirth, and orgasm. In these states, we focus our attention in a
different way than in ordinary consciousness. Thoughts, feelings,
sensations, and intuitions interconnect to bring us new information
and to facilitate healing and understanding of ourselves and of life
itself.[15]

Often written about as altered states of consciousness, nonordinary states are states of awareness and perception in an individual that differ substantially in subjective or objective observa-
tion from the general norms for that individual.[16] The states of
consciousness in which these intense experiences arise are known
by various names: therapeutic breakthroughs, abreaction, regression, altered states, shamanic states, ecstatic states, and peak experiences. I have chosen the term *nonordinary states of consciousness* because it is a broad, nonjudgmental term which includes any
state of consciousness characterized by a heightened sensitivity
and awareness and some of the specific phenomena described later
in this chapter.

Clients in ordinary states of consciousness

In most cases, when a client comes into therapy, talks to a masseuse at the beginning of a massage, or speaks to a minister or meditation teacher about her spiritual direction, she is more open, more vulnerable, and more in touch with her inner feelings and sensations than she is ordinarily. Usually, this openness is still on the "ordinary" side of the consciousness continuum. The client has her eyes open, she is verbal, she is fairly clear about who she is, where she is, why she is there, what she does and does not want, and how long she has been in the session. In general, an ordinary state of consciousness looks like this:

Ordinary State of Consciousness

⟶

Ordinary State of Consciousness   Nonordinary State of Consciousness

■ Is in touch with consensus
   reality

■ Talks easily

■ Has eyes open

■ Has clear sense of time,
   self, and others

■ Is cognizant of present
   surroundings

Nonordinary states in ordinary therapy

Any good therapy involves a nonordinary state of consciousness at some time and to some degree. Therapy is about change, and profound change involves a radical shift in self-view, worldview, or spiritual understanding. Nonordinary states allow ingrained habits of thought, feeling, perception, and understanding to recede, diffuse, and break down as necessary so that people can find new understanding and reclaim disconnected parts of themselves.

Over and over again, those individuals who are changing and developing realize they have contained themselves in too small a cognitive or emotional box. Each time they realize they are in a box fashioned of their beliefs and fears, they struggle to find greater freedom. In the moment of breaking out of the smaller box, they enter a nonordinary state which is often a moment of profound experience in therapy. This moment is accompanied by a rush of emotion and greater vulnerability. It is a time of disorientation when they find themselves outside their familiar, small reference points and in an unknown larger framework.

I am writing primarily about intense, prolonged, spontaneous or intentionally induced nonordinary states of consciousness. However, many of the concepts in this book apply also to these therapeutic moments of profound change in ordinary therapy, even though these moments are not identified commonly as nonordinary states.

In addition to peak nonordinary moments of finding a new conceptual frame of reference, momentary nonordinary states occur also in healing from trauma. Most wounding (mental, physical, emotional, or spiritual) involves nonordinary states at the time of the injury or trauma so the client must relive to some degree a nonordinary state during the healing process as well. Intense pain, fear, guilt, or shame is often enough to catapult a person into feelings and frames of mind which do not seem *ordinary* to the client.

Inner child work, in a sense, is nonordinary reality because regression is often part of that work. Sudden grief or loss also can precipitate a nonordinary state because outer circumstances disturb our beliefs about "the way it is." Earthquakes enable people to realize the lack of solidity of the earth and the impermanence of things on which they thought they could rely. The death of a friend awakens a client to his own mortality. Each of these events may require us to expand our mental constructs about who we are and what the world is. In the moment of expansion, we almost always enter a nonordinary state of consciousness. Some are mild *ah hah!* experiences. Some are momentous times in which we fundamentally change our values and lives.

Mild Nonordinary State of Consciousness

-->

Ordinary State of Consciousness   Nonordinary State of Consciousness

- Is in reverie

- Has ability to easily
  report verbally

- Has ability to respond
  relatively quickly to questions
  or direction

- Has ability to relatively
  quickly re-focus or switch to
  ordinary reality

Stephen Wolinsky, author of *Trances People Live*, points out that while trance may be deliberately induced by the therapist, the symptom which brings the client to therapy in the first place (e.g., depression) is itself a trance. It is a trance sustained by deep trance phenomena such as negative hallucination (e.g., not seeing positive aspects of the current situation) and pseudo-orientation in time (e.g., feeling as if a feared future were happening now.) Therapy, Wolinsky says, offers an opportunity to awaken from trance.[17] Perhaps we could consider nonordinary states of consciousness to be the doorways to awakening from the normal trance of daily life in which our awareness is narrowed and dulled.

The nonordinary state allows our higher Self's awareness to penetrate and permeate the trance sleep of our symptoms and behavior patterns. When we are "awake" in this way we are usually in a nonordinary state. Conversely, when we induce a nonordinary state, we often find ourselves more open and welcoming to such awareness.

Deep Nonordinary State of Consciousness

————————————————————►

Ordinary State of Consciousness   **Nonordinary State of Consciousness**

- Has difficulty in functioning in an ordinary way

- Has less access to reference points in ordinary reality

- Has less ability to express the experience in words

- Experiences time distortion

- Has access to deeper levels of healing

- Has access to mystical states

- Expresses self more spontaneously through movement and sound

---

Ordinary and nonordinary states exist on a continuum. As a client makes the transition from ordinary reality to nonordinary reality in mid-continuum, he focuses on his inner reality but has easy access to ordinary reality at the same time.

Reverie, guided relaxation, and most massage produce *nonordinary* states at the more *ordinary* end of the continuum. Although a client is aware of an inner reality in these states, he is usually able to report orally what is happening, respond relatively quickly to verbal questions or direction, and re-focus easily on the present, outer reality.

Usually, when a person moves farther into the nonordinary state, the person may have less access to ordinary reference points and may feel less able to talk. Time may seem distorted, persons and places may be confused, and inner and outer reality may blend in such a way that it is temporarily difficult for the person to function in an *ordinary* way.

Simultaneously, the person may gain more access to deeper levels for healing. She may reconnect to parts of her own experience from which she had become disconnected. She may more easily feel her association to universal experience—to other people, to animals and plants, to Earth, and to God as she understands God. Ancient peoples have long known the value of these deep states for physical and emotional healing, establishing inner and outer harmony with oneself and one's relations, and finding one's sense of life's purpose.

For the purposes of this book, I will use the term *nonordinary state of consciousness* to describe the deeper nonordinary experience (see chart, above) that occurs in various kinds of therapeutic or caregiving situations. In therapy, people move into nonordinary states in two ways—spontaneously or by therapeutic induction.

Spontaneously occurring nonordinary states of consciousness[18]

Sometimes people find themselves moving spontaneously into nonordinary states. Some clients attribute this unplanned change in state to a catalytic event such as the death of a loved one, loss of home or employment, loss of other identity, illness, near death experience, or other life-changing circumstance. Others may experience a powerful, nonordinary state during an intense sexual encounter, childbirth, or physical trauma. Some may have taken psychedelic drugs recreationally and found themselves beginning an ongoing spiritual emergence process in their lives after an unexpected, profound shift in perception. Still others feel the nonordinary state come upon them without precipitation by any particular life event but seemingly because the inner healing process needs to begin its work at that time. Some inner wisdom helps them let go of reality as they have known it, in order to expand their understanding of themselves and their world.

Nonordinary State Experiences

- Biographical flashbacks
- Trauma re-enactment
- Reliving birth
- Emotionally charged imagery
- Psychic and intuitive flooding
- Shamanic trance
- Past life flashbacks
- Intense energy release
- Out of body experiences
- Near death experiences
- Deep relaxation and peace
- Meditation and deep concentration
- Contact with archetypal realms
- Unitive or cosmic consciousness
- UFO abduction
- Multiplicity

Some caregivers might say they do not use any special techniques to induce nonordinary states of consciousness and therefore that the following material does not apply to their work. However, a portion of their clients will probably at some time have at least a few of the above experiences spontaneously. Caregivers working with clients, patients, students, or spiritual seekers may find it useful to be able to recognize and work with people who suddenly find themselves in the midst of spontaneous experiences listed above.

Biographical flashbacks

In a biographical flashback, a person relives an unfinished piece of his history. For some reason he was not able in that particular, personal historical moment to fully feel. He could not experience his joy, rage, fear, remember his own actions at that time, or feel the full extent of his pain, ecstasy, or other sensation. In the biographical flashback, he gets a hint of the therapeutic work he has yet to do. He may be able to complete a piece of his unresolved biography.[19]

Trauma re-enactment

Trauma re-enactment or abreaction involves more extensive reliving than the flashback. The person has the opportunity to reconnect her emotions, cognition, sensation, and intuition, and to release long-held energies in the mind, the emotional and physical bodies, and the spirit.

Reliving birth

Trauma re-enactment can include the birth trauma. Reliving birth enables a person to fully experience her own organism's first and perhaps most powerful imprint or patterning in dealing with major change.[20] Healing and understanding at this level has a domino healing effect on many similar situations that occurred after birth. Reliving birth is not always traumatic. The struggle for survival during labor and delivery are often traumatic, but someone can experience the time before labor begins as a wonderful fetal period of cosmic connection. A person can also experience birth itself as success, reunification, and loving reception.

Emotionally charged imagery

A person experiencing emotionally charged imagery may or may not understand cognitively the connection between symbols and images that arise in her mind and her strong emotional responses. These responses can result in deep grieving, animal-like rages, or profound joy and tranquillity. The nonordinary state seems to allow these images to arise and triggers deep emotional release without necessarily requiring an explanation. Intuitive flooding (psychic flooding) is emotionally charged imagery which seems to have its source outside the personal psychology, although the client can often relate the content also to her personal history. In a psychic opening, a person may feel the pain of those at war across the sea, may have precognitive experiences, or may be unusually receptive or psychic with those around her.

Shamanic trance

Shamanic trance takes many forms. A person takes shamanic "journeys" into nonordinary reality in order to seek wisdom or healing. Shamanic experiences may include channeling "spirits" in the mind or body or seeking prophetic visions. A shamanic experience may entail experiences of destruction and rebirth (such as feeling one's own flesh being stripped to the skeleton and being rebuilt with new or "spiritual" flesh), and cellular healing. Other shamanic experiences involve *soul retrieval*,[21] and receiving the guidance of numinous beings and power animals.

Past life flashbacks

Past life flashbacks occur in much the same way as biographical flashbacks, but they are of a former time and place. The person identifies with a character in that setting and has the sense that he is re-experiencing a situation he once lived as a different person. Regardless of whether or not one believes in reincarnation, these images are often powerful, healing metaphors for the situations found in the person's present life.

Intense energy release phenomena

Yogic mystical literature describes various intense energy release phenomena. These are phenomena that occur when the dormant evolutionary life energy (*kundalini*) rises from its resting place at the base of the spine and makes its way toward spiritual consciousness at the crown of the head. The yogic texts describe many physical and emotional phenomena that may include the temporary symptoms of illness or pain, such as feelings of burning, cold, unusual sweating, chest pain, and neurological symptoms. Spontaneous physical movements may occur, such as uncontrollable shaking, sudden jolts, and vibratory sensations. People experiencing energy release may have vivid visual images and see lights or colors. Spontaneous crying, laughing, chanting, toning, or other sounds may arise.[22]

Out of body experiences

Out of body experiences may occur as part of other experiences (such as shamanic and hypnotic) or by themselves. Some part of the person's consciousness separates from the body and travels outside the body. The consciousness remains, although it experiences itself as separate from the body. There are many examples in the literature of persons looking down at their own bodies from some vantage point on the ceiling.[23] Sometimes the person does not know what happened while he was out of body. He may realize he was "out" when he re-enters the body with a jolt or shock. He may feel a short period of physical "paralysis" as the consciousness and the body re-connect.

Near death experiences

Near death experiences occur when a person begins the death process. At some point the movement toward dying reverses and the person returns to life. Those who study near death experiences find that many different people have similar reports. As they approach death, they often move quickly down a tunnel, see light of indescribable beauty, meet deceased loved ones or spiritual figures, experience a profound review of the life they have lived, and receive a message that it is not time for them to die.

Near death experiences happen due to illness, accident, shock, or coma. A person who returns to ordinary life from such an experience may feel her life has changed profoundly. A person often reports feeling a greater sense of purpose and more commitment to loved ones than before the experience.[24]

Deep relaxation and meditation

Deep relaxation, peace, and various states of meditation are also nonordinary state experiences. These may occur at the close of a particularly deep resolution of therapeutic material or during out of body experiences or shamanic journeys. Hypnosis and guided relaxation can induce such deep relaxation and peaceful states.

Contact with archetypal realms and unitive experiences

Contact with archetypal realms can occur during many of these other experiences. The person communicates with or experiences actually becoming an archetypal figure such as a power animal, a god or goddess, or an element such as wind, water, or fire. These are often peak experiences, described in the mystical literature of all religions. A person may contact archetypal realms or have mystical, peak experiences and thereby find personal answers to existential questions and a depth of personal meaning not possible to achieve in an ordinary state of consciousness.[25] Unitive experiences are those in which the person feels a sense of merging with everything or identifying with a cosmic consciousness. (See also *Chapter 11*.)

UFO abduction experiences

I have included this category of nonordinary experience because the people who report abductions by aliens experience symptoms of post-traumatic stress disorder for which they may seek therapy or spiritual counseling. They experience being the subjects of research experiments and often have black-outs or loss of time. When such a client does seek therapy, the therapist usually employs hypnosis (an induced nonordinary state) to gather information and to help the client deal with his symptoms.

People who report encounters with aliens also experience phenomena and experiences for which there is no explanation within the current understanding of physics. These include experiencing other realities "beyond the veil" of this one, returning to a "source of being" or cosmic consciousness, and shape-shifting in the shamanic sense of becoming animals or animals reshaping themselves into aliens.[26] I describe in this chapter some of these kinds of experiences also as non-UFO, shamanic, or unitive consciousness experiences.

UFO abduction experiences have been reported in increasing numbers since 1961. They have been reported by people from all walks of life and geographical areas. The stories of many of these people are similar. The abduction experiences are a kind of nonordinary state which crosses the line between inner, nonordinary reality and outer, physical/material reality. The inner experience of abductees is often "corroborated" in physical reality by actual marks or symptoms or by the synchronistic, identical experiences of other abductees who were unknown to each other at the time of the experiences.

Harvard psychiatrist John E. Mack writes in his book *Abductions*, "We do not know what an abduction really is—the extent, for example, to which it represents an event in the physical world or to which it is an unusual subjective experience with physical manifestations."[27] What is clear, however, is that people are reporting these experiences and that this represents a phenomenon that scientists in the fields of both psychology and physics cannot conscientiously ignore.

Multiplicity

We can also classify some of the states that occur during the switching between alters in clients who have multiple personalities (sometimes diagnosed as Multiple Personality Disorder or MPD), and in the alters themselves, as spontaneous nonordinary states of consciousness.

Multiplicity is a condition that is usually created during extreme sexual, physical, and emotional abuse. A person under this kind of severe pressure escapes from pain, terror, and humiliation by creating alters, which are other personalities or fragment personalities. These alters distribute among themselves a collective burden which is too great for one personality to bear. Alters can vary in age, sex, and all personality characteristics. Some alters even have different medical conditions than the others which inhabit the same body. Some of these alters dissociate entirely and exist in a disembodied state. From this vantage point they usually continue to affect the other alters and the host personality. Some of the alters have easy access to transpersonal, nonordinary states of consciousness which provide a haven from the abusive, physical (ordinary) reality.[28]

Children and adults who have been ritually abused experience nonordinary states. Some unwittingly create nonordinary states in themselves as a refuge from what is happening. Some compartmentalize the abuse separately from their ordinary life to avoid intolerable cognitive dissonance. Ritual abuse perpetrators are reported to induce counter-therapeutic nonordinary states in their victims through drugs, hypnotic suggestion (programming), intolerable psychic or physical pain, or a combination of these means. Some ritual abuse cults intentionally may create multiple personalities in their members in order to control the members or use these alters for certain functions in ritual.[29]

Inducing nonordinary states therapeutically

Another means of entering nonordinary states is therapeutic induction. The therapist or professional facilitator employs a particular technique with clear intention to assist a person into a

Techniques for Inducing Nonordinary States

- Breathwork
- Massage and bodywork
- Acupuncture
- Process-Oriented techniques
- Movement and art therapy
- Music therapy
- Dreamwork
- Bioenergetic therapy
- Network Chiropractic
- Guided imagery
- EMDR
- Meditation and prayer
- Hypnosis
- Drumming
- Chanting and Singing
- Sweat lodge
- Soul retrieval
- Ingestion of sacred plants
- Fasting
- Vision quests

nonordinary state of consciousness in order to facilitate her healing process. All of the above spontaneous experiences are also possible within induced nonordinary states. Therapists, spiritual leaders, and facilitators now use various induction techniques regularly. The list in this chapter includes some of the more common techniques which are used educationally, therapeutically, and spiritually.

Breathwork

Breathwork is a term most commonly used to describe a group or individual process that uses accelerated breathing. Breathwork often combines with other techniques such as sonic driving (rhythmic beat), energy release work, art work, and guided relaxation. Holotropic Breathwork™, Integrative Breathwork, and ReBirthing are three well-known processes that use accelerated breathing as the catalyst for the nonordinary state. All of the experiences described above can happen with great intensity during a breathwork experience.[30] Some therapies, such as Reichian Therapy and Bioenergetic Analysis, also use modification of the breath to deepen the therapeutic process.

Massage

Massage promotes relaxation and dreamy reverie. The rhythmic movements and deep releasing pressure of various forms of bodywork can also trigger profound nonordinary states. The tissue can release its memories along with its tensions. As the muscles and joints expand their capacity for motion, the bodymind often re-connects motion with emotion. Many bodywork systems, such as Rosen work, Hakomi, Lomi body work, Feldenkrais, Rolfing, and Trager work, pay special attention to the breath to evoke the deeper awareness that occurs in nonordinary states.

Acupuncture

Acupuncture is especially known for the deep trance state often induced by the needles. During this state of nonordinary consciousness, energies are balanced and redirected and toxins are more easily eliminated. Occasionally the needles will tap into some process of the psyche (biographical, perinatal, or transpersonal) and the person on the table will have one of the nonordinary state experiences discussed previously.

Process-Oriented therapy

Many kinds of process therapy (movement and art therapy, dreamwork, sand play, Arnold Mindell's Process-Oriented Therapy techniques called processwork or dreambodywork, bioenergetic therapy, and gestalt therapy) can lead a person into a nonordinary state of consciousness. Sometimes these states are light trance states and the person feels as if she has a foot in both worlds. With this flexible posture, she moves fairly easily in and out of ordinary and nonordinary spaces. Occasionally the process will deepen so that the person is completely engaged in the nonordinary reality. When that happens any of the nonordinary experiences may occur in varying degrees of intensity.

Music therapy

Music has been used since ancient times as a way to induce nonordinary states and to promote healing. Drumming, chanting, and rattling have been used for centuries not only because they facilitate accelerated breathing without a pause but because they harmonize the energies (heartbeat and other pulses) present in the body of the individual. In a group, this harmonizing of bodily rhythms creates a special state of consciousness where we can commune together.

Mickey Hart, in *Drumming on the Edge of Magic,* speculates that the rhythms of the drum let us fall into a state of receptivity that could be the beginning of trance. This rhythmic entrainment was the vehicle used by shamans (tribal psychological and spiritual healers) to move into the spirit world.[31]

In modern times some therapists and healers are now using the many forms of music, including the vibration and pitch of toning, to consciously change state, attitude, and mood, and to promote healing. One teacher on the forefront of this kind of music education is Don Campbell. His Institute for Music, Health, and Education[32] trains healers and educators in the power of sound to bring about physical, mental, and spiritual well-being.

Network Chiropractic

Developed by Dr. Donald Epstein, Network Chiropractic is a particular system of chiropractic work. Network Chiropractors believe that the individual who is clear of interference in his nervous system has a freer connection among his emotional, physical, and spiritual aspects. By adjusting the spine, Network Chiropractors remove interference in the nervous system.[33] These chiropractors often work on several patients on tables in the same room, moving among them to correct spinal subluxations. It is not uncommon for various nonordinary state phenomena to occur during this energy-releasing work.

Guided states

With the techniques of hypnosis, guided relaxation, Eye Movement Desensitization Response (EMDR), and meditation, caregivers intentionally induce trance states. Stephen Wolinsky writes, "Trance is characterized by a narrowing, shrinking, or fixating of attention."[34] A hypnotist may suggest age regression so that the client relives specific early childhood experiences. Some hypnotists now specialize in past-life regression, in which the client is regressed in age to a time before birth in order to know the karma or personal myth that precedes or informs this lifetime.

There are many other uses of hypnosis as well. In the nonordinary state of hypnotic trance, the client may tap into any experience in the biographical, perinatal, or transpersonal areas. Sometimes these journeys are intentionally focused by the hypnotist and sometimes the experiences arise spontaneously once the client has entered a trance state.

EMDR

EMDR (Eye Movement Desensitization and Reprocessing) is a rapid eye movement technique. It is noted for achieving fast results in healing the effects of trauma.[35] The eyes of the client follow the rapid hand movements of the therapist. This induces a trance conducive to reintegration of images, body sensations, and verbal thoughts connected to the trauma. Some of the nonordinary experiences already discussed (particularly emotionally charged imagery, biographical flashbacks, strong sensory or kinetic experiences, and deep relaxation) are common in EMDR sessions.

Meditation and prayer

Spiritual traditions have practiced achieving nonordinary states through meditation and prayer for as long as we have records of human life. Meditation and prayer experiences range in intensity from more focused concentration of attention to deep nonordinary states. Some long-time meditators are surprised when their formerly quiet meditation becomes active and vocal (as in the kundalini experiences described above). Meditators also can have any of the other nonordinary state experiences described above.[36]

Hypnosis

Hypnosis is the technique for inducing nonordinary states which Western psychology has accepted and used longest. In hypnosis the therapist focuses the attention of the client more narrowly than usual. Rather than having a broad orientation to reality, the client's attention rests on certain designated factors.[37] Therapists use hypnosis for the purpose of facilitating age regression and trauma abreaction,* pain and anxiety management, and behavior change. Some hypnotherapists specialize in what they call past-life regression in which a client remembers an identity in another time and place in order to shed light on their current life situation.

---

*An episode of emotional release or catharsis associated with the bringing into conscious recollection previously repressed unpleasant experiences.

Recently, there has been revived interest in transpersonal hypnosis. In transpersonal hypnosis, the hypnotist acts as a collaborator with the client for the client's transcendence. This kind of exploration of peak or mystic experiences through induced hypnosis was first identified as "being-hypnosis" by Abraham Maslow. Maslow contrasted "being-hypnosis" with "striving hypnosis" or "role-playing hypnosis" which is more goal directed and behavior oriented.[38]

Shamanic techniques

Shamanism uses time-tested techniques by which ancient peoples entered nonordinary states individually and as communities. Drumming regulates the pulses of the body and, like the sonic driving of biofeedback machines, induces the brainwave frequencies of alpha, theta, and delta states. Drumming attunes the participants in soul retrieval, shamanic drum journeying, and other group ritual. Chanting to the drumbeat regulates the breath which helps produce a nonordinary state.

Other techniques used to induce nonordinary states include sweat lodges, which induce the nonordinary state through extreme temperature and fasting, which is one of the most powerful ways to propel oneself into a nonordinary state. These techniques are often used in combination as well as alone. Some therapists are trained, (*e.g.*, the Harner Method Shamanic Counseling),[39] to use methods such as divination and soul retrieval for various specific healing purposes. Westerners have adapted many of these practices and are using them in therapy as well as in workshops all over the world.

The people of many ancient cultures ritually ingested particular plants which they considered sacred. These sacred substances have the ability to induce powerful nonordinary states. Some tribal societies carry on these traditions even today.[40] Much research in the 1950s and 1960s strongly pointed to the considerable healing potential of these substances.[41] They were found valuable for the treatment of addiction,[42] for fear and pain in terminal cancer patients, and for mental illness.[43] Despite such promising early work, there was a political moratorium in the United States on further research with these substances. It was not until 1990 that research began again in the United States. At that time research was also underway in Germany and Switzerland.[44] Rick Doblin of the Multidisciplinary Association for Psychedelic Studies writes that there have been some hopeful signs in the mid-1990s that government-approved research into the therapeutic use of these valuable substances may begin again in the United States.[45]

Vision quests, in which seekers spend a day or several days alone in nature hoping for a vision or particular guidance in their lives, are potent consciousness-changing experiences. Vision quests may combine various, time-honored, consciousness-altering techniques that work synergistically to deepen the nonordinary state. Some of these methods are sleep deprivation, fear and challenge, extreme temperatures, fasting, drumming, sensory deprivation, or ingestion of sacred plants.

The role of awareness of client and caregiver in nonordinary states

The difference between psychosis and a nonordinary state of consciousness is sometimes difficult to discern from the outside. The dramatic symptoms may be similar or different in each state. The client's awareness of the process and his cooperation with it may be a key indicator that the client is in a transformative rather than pathological process. Generally psychosis is a defensive pattern functioning to keep awareness and pain at bay. Nonordinary states, on the other hand, are openings for change and growth. Those experiencing nonordinary states are usually aware of the process they are undergoing and in some sense welcome the awareness and change that is happening.

Awareness also plays a key role in trauma abreaction. It is not useful to relive traumas without awareness. To relive a trauma without awareness is to re-traumatize oneself. This is *not* healing. Most states of nonordinary consciousness are induced within a set (the client's mental context for the session) and a setting (the physical and emotional context for the session) designed to enhance awareness. Awareness is not necessarily understanding or insight. For example, the physical body or the emotions can be aware, without cognitive awareness. Awareness at any level, with or without insight, has a developmental and healing impact on the client.

Nonordinary state experiences without awareness do not always allow healing and growth. Party use of LSD exemplifies this. LSD might catalyze important psychological material, but the set may prohibit understanding of the experience and the setting may discourage complete experience of these emotions, images, and sensations. Lacking a safe setting, the person may feel instead the need to repress or distract herself from her inner material in order to protect herself and to interact with others at the party.

Arnold Mindell, a Jungian psychoanalyst who developed his own unique processwork technique, works with clients' *dreambodies* in nonordinary states which he calls *altered states* or *extreme states*. He describes the function of the therapist as helping to make an awareness bridge for the client and compares it to the work of the shaman. The therapist does this by witnessing, mirroring, and by not allowing herself to be drawn into the client's trance.[46] "Shamans heal by reminding you of the dreamingbody. They model awareness and the dance of the spirit."[47] The attention and awareness of the therapist help the client to tune in to that part of himself which is always aware. He can then experience the past in the present and become free of it through present awareness, rather than merely repeating the past in a loop without awareness.

In trauma recovery, healing cannot occur without awareness of the bigger picture. The client does not simply relive the abuse or traumatic incident, but brings greater awareness to the scene. She may feel not only her emotions and sensations from the past, but the motivations and emotions of her perpetrator in the past. She also brings awareness to the relationship between that past trauma and her present life.

Transcendence, or spiritual liberation, of course, cannot occur without awareness either. Jack Kornfield, Buddhist spiritual teacher and clinical psychologist, in his book, *A Path with Heart*, cautions against emphasizing the nonordinary experiences of meditation, rather than awareness of the process as a whole. He writes, "When such [nonordinary] experiences arise, the practitioner's primary responsibility is to open to the experience with a full awareness, observing and sensing it as part of the dance of our human life."[48]

3

The Special Needs of Clients in Nonordinary States of Consciousness

*As a midwife to the
psychospiritual, developmental process
occurring in nonordinary states,
the caregiver permits, protects, and ushers forth
that which wants to happen of its own accord.*

—K.T.

Categories of ethical issues

In this book, there are two broad categories of ethical issues discussed. The first category is one in which the ethical standards are common to both ordinary and nonordinary states of consciousness therapy. This category contains ethical guidelines useful to both states. The issues in this category do seem to need more emphasis, however, in order to work with intense and profound states in a conscientious way.

The second category contains ethical issues which do not usually apply to practicing therapy with clients in ordinary states of consciousness but may be important to consider when inducing nonordinary states in clients. The issues in this category may also apply to working with clients who have entered spontaneously into nonordinary states and are having intense and profound experiences. These clients include those who experience intense perception-shifting moments in the course of ordinary therapy.

Ethics common to all work with clients

In both states of consciousness, a therapeutic contract is a good basis upon which to proceed. Included in the contract are such things as a description of the procedures to be used and the boundaries and limits that are being set for the protection and integrity of both.

Caregiver and Client Agreements Common to All Therapeutic Work

- Caregiver will do no harm

- Caregiver will keep confidentiality

- Caregiver will get informed consent from client

- Both will tell the truth to each other

- Both will keep agreements with each other

- Client will do no violence to persons or property

- Both will not act sexually or romantically with each other

- Both will agree clearly on time, place, duration of session, and fee

---

These boundaries may include that both client and caregiver will tell the truth and keep their agreements with each other, that the client will do no violence to persons or property during the sessions, that there will be no sexual or romantic behavior between the caregiver and client, that the caregiver will cause no harm, and that the caregiver will maintain confidentiality with regard to the sessions (except for mandatory reporting laws). Client and caregiver make clear agreements with each other about time, place, duration, and fee for the therapy. The caregiver provides the client with enough information about the type of therapy she will use so that the client can give informed consent to the treatment process.

Ethical issues pertaining specifically to clients in nonordinary states

Therapists often feel that they will have no difficulty maintaining ethical conduct in therapy. Yet nonordinary states can seem to change those easily avoidable pitfalls to invisible, deep quagmires. Such a disturbing metamorphosis in the situation occurs because of the intensity of the work, the depth of transference and unacknowledged counter-transference, the greater suggestibility of the client, and other factors which I will discuss.

Special situations arise in nonordinary states that are different from those in ordinary states of consciousness. Some of these situations have already given rise to lawsuits, controversy among therapists, and misunderstandings between therapists and their clients. "False memory syndrome" is a term used by some clients, or their families. The term describes the recovery of memories during therapy and the subsequent belief that these memories were fabricated and implanted by the therapist.

Using the example of memory retrieval

Retrieval of memories of childhood abuse offers a good illustration of an experience in a therapeutic nonordinary state. It provides an example for discussing the general ethical issues of therapeutically induced nonordinary states of consciousness.

Early memories often return, or become more vivid, during a nonordinary state of consciousness. The nonordinary state may occur in a therapist's office, in a public breathwork workshop, in a men's drumming workshop, on a massage table, or in a minister's office. Wherever it occurs, regression and abreaction are possible.

The elements of those ethical issues and needs which might arise in any profound client experience and which are the primary substance of this book are: (1) The need for an expanded paradigm which can contain the kinds of experiences people have in nonordinary states; (2) The special competencies and training needed by someone working with clients in nonordinary states; (3) The greater need for a safe setting for clients experiencing nonordinary reality; and (4) The potential for stronger, more subtle, and more complicated transference and countertransference.

Ethical Issues in Working with Profound Client Experiences and Nonordinary States

- The need for a therapeutic paradigm that encompasses the phenomena of nonordinary states

- The special competencies required of a therapist or facilitator working with nonordinary state experiences

- The greater need for a safe setting

- The potential for stronger and more complicated transference and countertransference

---

Using an expanded therapeutic paradigm

Western psychology has concerned itself primarily with a person's historical development from infancy to the present and with her relationship to self and others. When clients report experiences outside the scope of the normal consensus about material reality, they run the risk of being labeled delusional or disordered.

When some modern psychiatrists in the 1950s discovered they could induce nonordinary states by administering a psychedelic substance, it was the beginning of consciousness expansion in modern times, not only for the individuals involved, but for the whole field of psychology. Many of the research subjects who took these substances had experiences that found no place in existing Western scientific concepts.

Stanislav Grof was one of these early psychiatric researchers. He carefully studied notes he had made while supervising approximately 5,000 LSD sessions in order to begin mapping the expanded territory of the psyche.

Grof found that, once subjects had entered a nonordinary state of consciousness, they had a variety of experiences. Many of these experiences took them beyond their biographical memory, beyond their personal identity, and beyond current place and time. Some subjects in these sessions were psychiatric patients, but many were considered normal and quite functional people in ordinary reality. Some subjects were professionals who were training to work with nonordinary states, others were dying of cancer, and still others were recovering from addiction. Subjects in all study groups, "normal" and "abnormal," experienced inexplicable energies, re-experienced their own births, visited archetypal realms, and gained access to information and understanding not available to them in ordinary consciousness or ordinary talk therapy.[49]

Observing this, Grof described two categories of nonordinary state experiences which expanded the psychological paradigm beyond the biographical domain. He called the two categories *perinatal* and *transpersonal*.[50] *Perinatal* described experiences surrounding the birth of the subject. *Transpersonal* described experiences beyond the personal identity, physical reality, and causal relationships.

Grof added to these categories the concept of a COEX system. A COEX is a *system of condensed experience*. In a COEX, biographical, perinatal, and transpersonal experiences are linked, usually by some element, sensation, or emotion common to all. Thus, in the nonordinary state a person may cough and choke, then re-experience elements of choking during birth (perinatal), or being choked by a mugger in adulthood (biographical), and past-life memories or identification with a dying animal struggling for breath (transpersonal). In this case both the choking *sensation* and the *emotional* fear of not being able to get the next breath link these powerful, simultaneous memories or images.

Perinatal and transpersonal aspects of early childhood memory retrieval

The potential for COEX experiences expands the psychological paradigm and thus the lens through which we examine the example of memory retrieval. The traditional model of psychology designates retrieved early childhood memories as either "true" or "not true." Regarding the earliest memories of infant abuse, doubters protest that a baby's brain is not prepared to store such memories. Such a model offers only two choices. The event of which there is memory either did or did not happen. If it did happen, the memory has either been retrieved or it has not been retrieved.

Some say all such repressed and subsequently retrieved "memories" are true. Others say these scenarios are not true because if true the person would have remembered these events all along. There is a third possibility, however which could be called variously narrative truth, poetic truth, or archetypal truth.

Donald P. Spence, author of *Narrative Truth and Historical Truth,* offers the thought to psychoanalysts that, "Something may become true simply by being put into words." He says that once we see the past in a particular manner, that way of viewing it or defining it *becomes* the past. He reasons that many of our preverbal experiences have no language assigned to them at the time. When certain language is assigned later, either by ourselves or by a caregiver, that expression defines the experience.[51]

When one can use poetic license in giving expression to preverbal experiences, one can take what Spence calls an *artistic* approach to understanding one's life, rather than an *archaeological* one.[52] It is easier to allow for artistic truth in personal history, if one's paradigm gives credence to the perinatal and trans-personal areas of experience as well as the biographical ones.

When we include the perinatal and transpersonal categories of experience, we find we can interpret memories in three ways. The first interpretation is that the retrieved memories actually happened, literally, as the client remembers them. The second interpretation is that they did not happen and they are being fabricated by a client who has conscious or unconscious motives for doing so. The third interpretation, possible with the expanded paradigm, is that certain "memories" may be real but constructed symbolically to represent various true feelings, sensations, or experiences. Personal myths in the form of such "memories" portray these real feelings, sensations, or experiences. Nonordinary experience, abreaction, and regression can be confusing combinations of these possibilities.

I have facilitated hundreds of nonordinary state (breathwork) sessions involving the reliving of childhood abuse. I believe that the body sensations and the meanings behind the images are always "true" in that participants are communicating an unequivocal reality of *experience*. They are *true* regardless of whether the life-historical events happened exactly as recalled. While we as care-givers rarely have the opportunity to know what actually happened so long ago, we can know intuitively from watching and feeling someone go through her pain and terror that she is re-experiencing some combination of abusive or invasive situations.

Personal myth and abuse memories

It is important that the paradigm in which we hold memory retrieval work does not limit its recognition of truth to literal and provable facts. Usually, we do not know what part of the memory retrieval is a literal representation of linear reality and what part is a mythical representation of reality. Myth is not fantasy, but rather a story which *represents* factual reality. Created from symbols and real events in the unconscious during nonordinary states of con-sciousness, myth may be part fact, part emotionally-charged symbol. The myth, like poetry, is created to represent the truth *more accurately than fact alone*.

Fantasy, on the other hand, is a purely creative invention. While it can be allegorical, fantasy is not easily confused with either subjective or literal reality. In language terms, myth is a combination of non-fiction and metaphor while fantasy is fiction and simile.

We know that different parts of the brain communicate in different ways. The left brain communicates more literally and verbally, the right brain more metaphorically and nonverbally or artistically. Both ways of communicating are useful, but we should not confuse the language of one with the language of the other. Like binocular vision, the use of both kinds of language can give depth to understanding a situation or subject.

We expand our working paradigm when we accept personal myth as a third choice beyond the notion of *it either happened or it did not*. Within an expanded paradigm, the client and therapist together investigate and validate the client's feelings, sensations, thoughts, and intuitions. Rebecca Davis, a social worker at a center for intensive memory retrieval work, is quoted as saying: "We never tell people that what you remembered is real. What is recovered is a mixture of what is real and what is not real—actual events, distortions, dream material, fantasies."[53]

Psychiatrist Judith Herman says, "Both patient and therapist must develop tolerance for some degree of uncertainty, even regarding the basic facts of the story."[54] Therapy focuses a client's attention back on the inner healing process, rather than on proving something to someone: therapist, family, society, or even a critical part of herself. If the client focuses outside herself, she may short-circuit her healing process. The Australian Psychological Society Limited writes in its "Guidelines Relating to the Reporting of Recovered Memories":

> *Psychologist should explore with the client the meaning and implications of the memory for the cli-*

ent, rather than focus solely on the content of the re-ported memory.[55]

There is no way of knowing for sure about the facts of child-hood sexual abuse. It may be wiser to let the inner healing process evolve for a while before the client takes any external action such as confronting a perpetrator or filing a lawsuit. The American Psychiatric Association published a *Statement on Memories of Sexual Abuse* stating:

> *It is not known how to distinguish, with complete accuracy, memories based on true events from those derived from other sources. . . . Some patients will be left with unclear memories of abuse and no corroborating information. Psychiatric treatment may help these patients adapt to the uncertainty regarding such emotionally important issues.*[56]

Two prominent psychiatrists and authors say they have experienced in dramatic ways the two sides of the question of false or accurate memory retrieval by clients. Colin Ross, M.D., who specializes in severe dissociative disorders and trauma recovery, and Stanislav Grof, M.D., whose life's work has been the exploration of nonordinary states in both clinical and educational sessions, each has had a client whom they believed was presenting mythical representations of childhood pain. Each of these two cases later presented dramatic external verification of factual accuracy. Their clients' "myths" became proven facts.

On the other hand, these two physicians both remember cases which appeared to contain factual histories of a certain type of childhood physical abuse. The clients, themselves, after several years of therapy, decided their stories of physical abuse were their own mythical representations of emotional abuse.[57] Again, the abuse was no less "real" for these clients, but they saw it differently at a later time from the way they first remembered it.

The perinatal influence in abuse memories

The perinatal and transpersonal levels of experience contribute additional complexity to the true or false controversy in the biographical domain.[58] As a culture, we do not even consider the possibility of birth trauma as a plausible explanation for signs of psychic and physical trauma. Until a person has had the opportunity to re-experience the birth trauma and feel personally its impact, birth is not usually given the credence it deserves. Birth is the first life-threatening trauma of the organism and its first experience of surrender and transformation (from a symbiotic, aquatic organism to an independent entity).

Birth as a reason for the body symptoms and unnamable emotions may seem too weird, too improbable. It is difficult for us in states of ordinary consciousness to identify with that fetus or newborn baby we once were. One man whom I know personally has a very different perspective on his own process now than when he began working with his childhood issues. He participated in many deep experiential sessions in nonordinary states for several years. In the early sessions, he became convinced that his mother had sexually molested him as an infant. As he continued his inner work, he encountered overwhelming rage and humiliation. He became so sure of the sexual abuse that he wrote a scathing letter to his mother. He broke off relations with her and did not speak to her for over two years, despite the fact that she protested vehemently that such events had never happened.

Several years later, he relived his birth in several nonordinary state sessions. The feelings of rage and humiliation began to seem more associated with his birth trauma than with some later event. Actual memories of the form of his molestation began to seem more like birth as well. He eventually wrote to his mother, rescinded his accusations, and reconciled with her. His current explanation is that he created a personal myth of infant sexual abuse to describe and explain the combination of abuse from the biographical and perinatal areas. His myth resulted from a mixture of severe emotional abuse during childhood and remembrance of his own birth trauma (bodily abuse while inside his mother).

The most common reason that birth is not considered as part of explanation of a COEX of abuse symptoms or imagery is that our culture does not think about birth in this way. As a culture we deny (until recently in some circles) that cellular memory and fetal consciousness are possible. When the therapeutic models expand to encompass the perinatal, both caregivers and clients have more options for understanding and supporting the healing process.

In addition to biographical and perinatal influences, the transpersonal level of experience may be a factor in memory retrieval. There are many doorways through which the transpersonal can enter a client's myth. All the events of past centuries and the art and religion of myriad cultures are available at the transpersonal level. People engage the transpersonal through the collective unconscious (*i.e.,* past life experiences, channeling, psychic impressions, and archetypal images). Even in a client's own biographical time, she may have empathized with the pain of another person to the extent that boundaries became indistinct. She internalized the other's experience as her own. If she heard or saw the abuse of a brother or sister, she may feel or remember the abuse as if it happened to her. Personal boundaries are diffused in the nonordinary state. One's sense of self and the self's experience can be very different than usual. The possibilities for the transpersonal involvement in a COEX are endless and often inexplicable.

Working with clients in these realms can be confusing. Clients can be having perinatal or transpersonal kinds of experiences or remembering events symbolically using perinatal and transpersonal imagery. This can be all the more confounding if we insist there is only one causal, concrete reality. This is why an expanded theoretical paradigm underlies ethical work with clients in nonordinary states of consciousness. Therapists can help clients frame their construction of personal history as personal myth. They can assist clients by encouraging them to take their time with the inner approach to healing. At the same time therapists can counsel caution about taking some action in the outer world as if the inner myth were completely factual. In most cases, childhood memories of abuse have a real basis in fact of some kind. In most of those cases, many of the memories are true literally, as remembered. But the main point of therapy and the caregiver's real business is assisting the client's inner healing, rather than acting to confirm facts, dates, and times.

Grof and others have been clear that nonordinary states and perinatal and transpersonal experiences are not pathological but actually are part of our normal human heritage. Furthermore, they have seen that these states and the experiences possible in them can be quite healing if the therapist is open to the nonordinary content.

The openness of the therapist is a key factor in how normal the client feels when having such experiences and whether the client can let the experiences develop and amplify. If the therapist views these states as pathological, the client will either abort the emerging process or internalize the criticism, feeling that at the deepest level of her being, something is wrong with her.

A therapist's theoretical elasticity in expanding to contain the actual details of a client's process determines how safe the client will feel to talk about or enter fully into these inner events. Mary Sykes Wylie writes:

> *Blind allegiance to a particular therapeutic model becomes an ethical failing when the therapist consistently gives more weight to the model than to what clients say they want and need.*[59]

There are instances in which clients are confused cognitively about what they want but often will express their needs verbally, bodily, and symbolically. Whenever the standard models of therapy do not serve the needs and experiences of clients, these are occasions for the pragmatic caregiver to take note and change what is not working.

Stanislav Grof had not developed his transpersonal maps of consciousness when he first encountered the experiences of nonordinary states in his early years of clinical psychiatry. In place of an expanded therapeutic paradigm, he held an unwavering stance as the scientific observer who clings to no model but observes, accepts, facilitates, and documents whatever truth is emerging in therapy. Fortunately for those of us who follow the early explorers, some of the previously uncharted territory of consciousness has been mapped and named by Western scientists Jung, Grof, Eliade, and others. We now have an expanded paradigm including not only biographical experiences, but also perinatal and transpersonal experiences. Such a model is large enough to encompass the experiences that are emerging in our clients' spontaneous and induced nonordinary states.[60]

Using the expanded paradigm in the context of religion

The need for an expanded paradigm in which to hold spontaneous, nonordinary states pertains to religion as well as psychology. People who report spontaneous nonordinary states often describe them as spiritual experiences. Spiritual experiences may be direct demonstrations of Spirit and may elucidate tenets of religious scripture.

Most writers of scripture and founders of religions based their writings on personal spiritual experience. When a client has a personal experience which feels spiritually significant to her, this may enrich her understanding of her own religion. Many in modern times report experiences which in traditional times were called mystical and seemed to happen only to a chosen few (at least in the history of today's great religions.) These personal spiritual experiences can expand a client's spiritual awareness beyond mere cognitive understanding of her religion.

Religious ceremony or spiritual retreats can trigger any of these experiences. Members and leaders of traditional Western religions may have to minister to parishioners or retreatants who move spontaneously into ecstatic states, feel powerful body energies, or experience psychic or emotional flooding.

There is precedent for such nonordinary states in the documented experiences of Jewish and Muslim prophets, Christian saints, and the mystics of Hinduism, Buddhism, and other religions. However, we do not expect these experiences to occur to ordinary people in most of today's temples and churches. Persons whose spontaneous ecstasy unfolds in the middle of most modern day church services might find themselves transported to a mental health crisis unit, rather than gently supported to feel fully and honor their direct spiritual connection. Religious officials and elders do not, for the most part, have the conceptual model or the training to help someone integrate this kind of important spiritual experience.

Some of the charismatic Christian churches and some Eastern religions take these experiences in stride. These religious cultures have an expanded paradigm which views direct spiritual experience in nonordinary states as normal and desirable. Their interpretation of scriptures includes, and even expects, these phenomena in the course of devotional, spiritual practice. Many of the phenomena listed above were first named and described in ancient Hindu, Taoist, and Buddhist texts. Even further back in time, ancient peoples, who did not even have a written language, have been well acquainted with the spiritual phenomena of nonordinary states.[61]

In those ancient times, the practice of religion and psychology were under the auspices of the tribal shaman. The shaman's most important professional credential was his or her proven facility in mediating between ordinary and nonordinary reality for the benefit of the community.[62] Modern psychology and modern religion have dissociated from each other; both have denied the reality and importance of nonordinary state experiences. The expanded paradigm implies healing of that schism and reclamation of the human capacities we have denied.

The need for special competencies in the therapist

Perhaps the most important ethical guideline with regard to inducing nonordinary states of consciousness in clients is that the therapist or facilitator practice only in her area of competence.

Hypnosis is an example of a technique which professional associations encourage their certified or licensed members not to use unless they have had specialized, adequate training and practice in the method.

Adequate training to induce nonordinary states of consciousness requires many personal therapeutic experiences *as the client* in nonordinary consciousness. Adequate training for the treatment of dissociative disorders, for the practice of Holotropic Breathwork, hypnosis, shamanic counseling, or EMDR require that the practitioner personally experiences nonordinary states of consciousness. Competency to facilitate these techniques requires personal familiarity with the kinds of experiences that may arise. It requires a thorough study of how those practices fit into a conceptual framework of therapy. It requires information about and practice in when and how to intervene in the nonordinary state experiences of others.[63] Stressing the importance of experiential training for therapists, Stanislav Grof writes:

> *If [caregivers] have not experienced deep letting go in death and rebirth type of sessions, if they have not experienced the choking struggle to breathe in reliving birth, if they have not felt the resolution of terror or deeply held body pain, then they are likely to freeze when encountering these things in participants' sessions. Their own fear, lack of personal knowledge, and insufficient faith in the process may communicate itself [to the client], preventing [the client] from going fully into the experience to complete it. This can happen even if the [caregiver] does nothing overtly to interfere with the [client's] process. Because of the nonordinary state of consciousness, [clients] are often unusually sensitive to the thoughts and emotions of [caregivers].*[64]

The length of time involved in such training (optimally two or more years) provides the opportunity to process and integrate the material that emerges during the personal experiential sessions.

Safe setting needs

Clients in nonordinary states are more suggestible and vulnerable. They are more likely to experience age regression, need therapeutic touch, and feel stronger personal desires, fears, and spiritual longings. They are generally unfamiliar with nonordinary states and may have great difficulty making the transition between ordinary and nonordinary reality when they are moving in either direction.

Safety Issues in Nonordinary State Work

- Close attention to set and setting
- Greater client suggestibility
- Attention to greater client security needs
- Informed consent issues
- Understanding regressed client's primary language
- Physical touch issues in the therapeutic relationship
- Integrating profound experiences
- Cognitive dissonance
- Somatic/psychospiritual crisis

Because of the expansive effect of nonordinary states on consciousness, clients are likely to have greater cognitive dissonance between this and their usual world view. They may have more need for an understanding, supportive network, and special back-up resources.

When so much change is happening internally, the client has a greater need to feel secure in the external environment and trust in the therapeutic relationship. This section covers some of these safety issues.

Somatic/psychospiritual crisis, otherwise called *spiritual emergency,* is also more likely because of the rapid developmental changes which often accompany nonordinary state work. Some examples are temporary dysfunction because of the overwhelming impact of cognitive dissonance, spontaneous energy release phenomena, or psychic flooding. The *Diagnostic and Statistical Manual* (DSM-IV), used by practitioners of mental health care in North America, lists *Spiritual or Religious Problem* as a diagnostic category which can include this kind of psychospiritual crisis.[65]

Close attention to set and setting

In any therapy session, the safety of the set and setting is important. In a session involving nonordinary states, the set and setting become crucial. The following definition of set and setting is taken from the discussion of client needs in a clinical LSD session. These definitions apply also to many types of sessions conducted in nonordinary states of consciousness, such as breathwork, hypnosis, EMDR, shamanic, *etc.*

> *The term "set" includes the expectations, motivations and intentions of the subject in regard to the session; the therapist's or guide's concept of the nature of the LSD experience; the agreed-upon goal of the psychedelic procedure; the preparation and programming for the session; and the specific technique of guidance used during the drug experience. The term "setting" refers to the actual environment, both physical and interpersonal, and to the concrete circumstances under which the drug is administered.[66]*

Societies that regularly use nonordinary states of consciousness as an integral part of their religious and healing rituals surround the nonordinary states of consciousness with special ceremony and symbol. The set is already deeply inculcated in the society's members by their mythical and spiritual tradition. The setting (*e.g.*, special songs, dances, costumes, quests, fasts, physical locations) for these states is quite different from that of the daily life of the people. Their cultural context leaves little room for confusion between the two realities.

In modern Western, therapeutic, nonordinary state sessions, the set includes informed consent (see below), including comprehensive information about the kinds of experiences that may occur, agreements about touch, sexual boundaries, non-violence, fees, time and duration of session(s), availability of the therapist for follow-up session(s), confidentiality, and therapeutic procedure.

Greater client suggestibility

The ethical issues regarding client suggestibility may be similar, but they are *quantitatively* different with clients who are in a different state of consciousness because of their profound experiences. Clients are more sensitive and more deeply vulnerable in these states than in ordinary states of consciousness. A therapist must be more vigilant not to impose her own values on the client. By asking leading questions, a therapist may be imposing her own values. By creating too focused a plan for the content of the nonordinary state session, or by analyzing or teaching a client who is in a nonordinary state (rather than merely facilitating), the therapist may be undercutting a client's own right to choose and discriminate. When a therapist imposes a certain perspective or direction on a suggestible client who is in a nonordinary state of consciousness, she may be interfering with the wiser agenda of the client's own inner healer. Brown and Fromm write about the client's state while under hypnosis:

> *The fact that a person in trance is more suggestible, less vigilant and thus perhaps also more vulnerable and less able to stand up for himself—places additional ethical requirements on the hypnotist to protect the hypnotized person from harm caused either*

by the hypnotist's suggestions or by the patient's own
strong affects that might overwhelm him.[67]

The factor of suggestibility has become a hot issue in therapy involving memory retrieval. Some say that by either agreeing or disagreeing with our patients' perceptions, we prevent the client from finding his or her own meaning to whatever may have really happened.

Harvard psychiatrist and author of books on trauma, Judy Lewis Herman, represents another view, usually espoused by therapists who treat incest victims and are often themselves survivors of child abuse:

The moral stance of the therapist is . . . of enormous
importance. It is not enough for the therapist to be
"neutral" or non-judgmental. The patient challenges
the therapist to share her own struggles . . . . The
therapist's role is . . . [to] affirm a position of moral
solidarity with the survivor.[68]

This solidarity can be appreciated as an important political function in a world which has only recently begun to address the extent of its abuse to its marginal groups, such as women and children. The statement does, however, imply suggestibility on the part of the client. The first viewpoint is that this kind of pro-active therapy could lead to a therapist's suspecting childhood abuse where it did not happen, or to a suggestible client producing "memories." More subtle invitations to the client may elicit responses and psychic material in order to please the therapist. A therapist's declaration of either a political position or a personal experience could lead a client who is uncertain about his hazy memories to become "clearer" about them in order to feel solidarity with his therapist.

A therapist may impose his values by omission as well as by commission—a kind of a therapeutic pocket veto. The client may understand from the therapist's silence that the client's experience is not acceptable for some reason.

Client Experiences Which a Caregiver Might Find Difficult to Affirm

- Past life experiences

- Ritual abuse

- Multiplicity

- Ecstatic states

- Out of body experiences

- Near death experiences

- Spiritual visions and concepts

- Kundalini symptomatology

- Shamanic healings

- Images from a religion other than the caregiver's religion

- Reliving birth

- UFO abductions

- Existential suicidality

The client may encounter a memory, a spiritual experience, or some other nonordinary reality which the therapist cannot validate. Past lives, ritual abuse, ecstatic states, spiritual concepts, emotionally charged images or themes from other religions, reliving birth, UFO abductions, or existential suicidality are some examples of experiences which may be difficult for a therapist to affirm.

The caregiver who operates from a paradigm which can encompass the phenomena of nonordinary states will be able to stay present for and to accept these experiences as well as the usual biographical ones. The caregiver who also has had strong experiential training in these realms will have become familiar with the terrain of nonordinary states of consciousness and will accept more easily the diverse possibilities without imposing his personal preferences.

Because of the client's increased suggestibility in the nonordinary state, there is the possibility of re-imprinting a client's distrust of her own intuition, feelings, senses, and memory more easily. On the other hand, there is more opportunity to empower her by trusting and affirming her inner, instinctive direction in therapy.

In any ordinary therapy session, there is always an interplay between directing the healing (treatment planning, suggestions, homework) and letting it unfold (non-directive therapy). In a session using nonordinary states, directive interventions are neither usually appropriate nor useful. They are more likely to be harmful. Holotropic Breathwork™ facilitators, for example, are trained specifically to refrain from intervention based on assumptions and analysis.[69] If they have been trained previously as therapists, they have to *un*learn their reflex to intervene. The therapist's role in nonordinary state sessions is to empower and to follow the client's process, not preempt it with the therapist's own agenda.

A caregiver's main job becomes like that of a midwife, rather than that of a strategist. As a midwife to the psychospiritual developmental process occurring in nonordinary states, the therapist permits, protects, and ushers forth that which wants to happen of its own accord. In hypnosis, guided imagery, shamanic extraction, or soul retrieval, there may be a definite agenda the therapist and client together have formulated while the client was still in an ordinary state of consciousness. Even in these cases, the therapist will be open to cues, which arise unpredictably in the nonordinary state, that the client's process wants to unfold in a different way than either of them had expected.

Greater client security needs

This subject is closely examined in Chapter 5. Clients who are stepping into the unknown territory of emotional intensity, retrieved memory, and profound spiritual experience need a safe setting. Even more than clients in ordinary therapeutic work, they need a context of trust in their environment and the person or persons who are with them. When these therapeutic agreements are clear and a therapeutic alliance feels trustworthy, the client can risk inner explorations.

Informed consent issues

Informed consent is the consent a client gives before she undergoes a therapeutic procedure. *Informed* consent implies that the client knows what the therapist will do and how the procedure is likely to affect her during and after therapy. In most ordinary state therapy, the therapist discusses with the client the way that she works, what will be expected of the client, and how the client is likely to benefit. Pope and Vasquez define informed consent this way:

> *Informed consent is an attempt to ensure that the trust required of the patient is truly justified, that the power of the therapist is not abused intentionally or inadvertently, and that the caring of the therapist is expressed in ways that the patient clearly understands and desires.*[70]

The therapist can include information to provide informed consent for nonordinary state work when she covers the ordinary information necessary for informed consent at the beginning of therapy. It often makes more sense to give this addendum later in therapy, before going forward with therapeutically-induced nonordinary state sessions.

At that time for example, the therapist can broaden the informed consent. The client who already understands the exceptions to confidentiality (such as state laws regarding the reporting of suspected child and elder abuse) or prevention of harm to self or others will then understand that these exceptions will apply also to information divulged while in the nonordinary state, as well as while in the ordinary state of consciousness. This may also help the therapist avoid a situation where the client claims he disclosed the information "unconsciously" (implication: against his will) while in a non-ordinary state.

The client contract can be expanded to include agreements with the client to the effect that he will not leave the premises during the session and will follow the instructions of the therapist without question in the event of an emergency (such as an earthquake or fire). The therapist can also make clear agreements about how she will handle hospitalization of the client in the event such twenty-four hour care should become necessary.

Examples of agreements a caregiver might make are:

■ *I will not violate your physical or sexual boundaries. You may ask for touch or holding if you want it. I will give it if I feel comfortable doing so.*

■ *If I think you might benefit from physical touch and you haven't asked me to touch you, I will ask you if it is all right to touch you before doing so.*

■ *I charge $50 an hour for ordinary therapy. This session may last from one and a half hours to two hours so the fee will be between $75.00 and $100.00.*

■ *I will be available tonight by telephone if you need to check in. I will check my messages every hour until 11 PM, so you can count on my calling you no later than one hour after you call me. We will see each other for a post-session session on Tuesday at 3 PM for one hour.*

Examples of agreements a client might make are:

■ *I understand that I can express rage and anger by using pillows and that I have full permission to ex-*

perience my anger if it comes up for me. I will be re-sponsible for not damaging persons or property while expressing my anger.

■ *I agree not to initiate any sexual interaction with my caregiver.*

■ *I will not leave the session until it is over (at the time we agreed upon.)*

■ *If the facilitator tells me there is an emergency (earthquake, fire, etc.), I will follow the directions of the facilitator.*

Informed consent is quantitatively different in a nonordinary state session because of the considerable preparation necessary before inducting a client into that state. It is qualitatively different because of the difficulty in describing to a client the experience of a nonordinary state of consciousness before he has experienced it. What is difficult to impart is the vividness of imagery, the depth of sensations and feelings, and the impact of these experiences on our self-concept and world view. Still, through reading or lecture, the client can become familiar enough with the inner cartography and its implications to give a properly informed consent.

When the nonordinary state arrives unexpectedly and sponta-neously, there may be no time to prepare the client when she is in an ordinary state of consciousness. The sudden disappearance of ordinary state communication can throw a caregiver off balance. In this case, at the earliest appropriate opportunity, the caregiver can state the pertinent ground rules and boundaries aloud, even if there is no perceivable response from the client. Kathryn Steele, director of a dissociative disorders unit in Atlanta, Georgia, uses a technique with multiples that she has finds effective, even though it seems to be one-way communication. Talking to all the alters sharing one body, she says *OK, everybody listen!* She then pro-ceeds to deliver her basic communications to all personalities in her client.[71] These are some examples of delivering important information to a client, even when the client is in a nonverbal, non-responsive, nonordinary state:

■ *This session will be over in one and a half hours. Then we will need to make a decision about whether you can function in ordinary consciousness again or whether you need continued care.*

■ *I have to leave you now for a little while, but this is my assistant, Chris. Chris will stay with you until I come back. I will be back.*

■ *I am your massage therapist. You are in my office. You are twenty-five years old. You are not three years old. Your father is not here. He cannot hurt you. You may be reliving the abuse, but it is not actually happening again. If there is anything you need, you can tell me or signal me.*

Understanding regressed client's primary language

If the client's primary spoken language is not understood by the caregiver, it is worth considering whether someone who speaks the client's language should be present for the session. In an age-regressed or deep emotional state, the client may have difficulty accessing a language learned later in life and may revert to the primary language. Without someone to understand his words and his needs, he may re-imprint neglect or misunderstanding. In a group context, such as breathwork or shamanic workshops, facilitators can usually arrange for someone who speaks the client's primary language to be present.

Physical touch issues in the therapeutic relationship

Touch is always a concern in therapeutic ethics. Some think a psychotherapist should never touch a client; others practice somatic psychotherapy. There are many stations in between. Both ends of the philosophical spectrum with regard to touch might claim that their positions are even more important to maintain when working with suggestible clients in therapeutically induced, nonordinary states of consciousness. The cautions against touching include the possibility of misunderstanding or confusion with transference or countertransference issues or enhanced sexual attraction.

The psychoanalytic view, for example, is that touching prevents awareness and healing. Psychoanalysts believe that a more primitive part of the client may well need physical touch. They believe, however, that psychotherapy will ultimately do her more good by helping her bring into words (*i.e.*, fully into adult consciousness) the intensity of her need and its sources. By verbalizing her needs and feelings, she will discover what has been blocking her from satisfying those needs in her daily life. Psychoanalysts would further contend that when physical touching by the therapist becomes a ritualized part of what is done in therapy, the client's needs are temporarily satisfied, but stay unconscious, resulting in chronic, persistent neediness.

Ordinary therapy may be very adequate most of the time without the therapist touching the client. There are times when a therapist should not touch a client; therefore, some have made it unethical ever to touch the client. This logic is flawed. It ignores those times when it is important to touch a client even during ordinary therapy. When we are working with a client in a nonordinary state of consciousness, there are some occasions when *not* touching the client would be unethical. Here are some examples of when this might be the case:

■ *The therapist provides nurturing touch to a client regressed to infancy and reliving the omission of maternal care. The client feels held and safe enough to feel grief about her early abandonment.*

■ *The trained facilitator provides some physical pressure, to amplify the body's memory. For example, at the client's request, the facilitator offers resistance by placing a hand on a painful spot on the client's arm. The client pushes against the facilitator's arm increasing the tension until the energy releases. The client may connect emotions and visual memories to such body symptoms.*

■ *A parishioner is experiencing existential fear and the caring hand of her minister helps her trust the process.*

If, for example, the client has regressed and has encountered the original trauma of not being touched and loved, she has an opportunity for a corrective experience. If she has summoned up the courage to ask to be held, only to have the facilitator or therapist refuse, this re-imprints the trauma of omission and rejection. If a trauma is being relived and remembered *cellularly*, the client may need touch to amplify the sensation or to assuage the fear of going through the process. Here are two examples, one in which touch assuaged the fear involved in reliving the trauma of omission (trauma from lack of care) and one in which touch amplified the trauma of commission (trauma from active harm):

■ *A young woman had had a difficult birth, followed by several weeks in an incubator, several months in the hospital separated from her mother and subsequent physical and sexual abuse in childhood. I held her in her regressed infant state through many breathwork sessions while she cried and cried. The nurturing allowed the woman to feel the intense fear and sadness of neglect and disconnection. When I last had contact with her, her breathwork sessions were beginning to include less helpless, infantile grief and more expressions of rage at her abuse as an older child.*

■ *In another breathwork session, a woman was reliving the trauma of repeated rape by several relatives when she was a tiny child. Her body remembered the bars of the bed's headboard pressing into her head. She placed the heel of my hand in that place on her scalp and pushed against it. This amplified the feeling in such a way that she could fully relive (abreact) the horrible scene.*

Touch is often an essential component in nonordinary state experiences, especially while assisting a client with closure. Whereas traditional therapy models may consider it harmful to touch the client, it may be harmful to a client in a state of nonordinary consciousness *not* to receive touch.

Mary Dale Scheller, a clinical social worker who also holds a massage license, writes about the need to integrate touch sometimes into verbal therapy, in order to *do no harm* therapeutically:

> *I believe a well-trained therapist should know some methods of body-oriented therapies that she could employ if needed, especially when working with clients who have body-based traumas. Moreover, clinicians concerned with the ethical and clinical issues of touch should be conversant in the harmful effects of the avoidance of touch along with the discussions of its use.*[72]

Certainly it is difficult to touch effectively and safely if the transference or countertransference issues include romance and sexuality, codependence, or hostility. But if these are not at issue in the therapeutic relationship or if they are handled by people with clear boundaries, then these concerns recede.

The question of appropriate touch is also less relevant if the work is done in a group setting. The issue of touching clients during a group Holotropic Breathwork session, for example, is different from the issue of touching clients during a private therapy session. Grof writes:

> *The problem of physical contact is significantly simplified by the fact that we almost always work in a group context. The reasons and rules for the use of intimate support are clearly explained and they are accepted by the group as part of the procedure. The*

*areas of the body that are being touched are deter-
mined by the inner process of the experient, not by
the choice of the sitter [the partner or facilitator in
attendance]. In addition, all that happens along these
lines happens publicly and under collective supervision of the group. This is a situation that differs
considerably from the context of individual work in
private practice.*[73]

The quality of touch is also an issue. When the therapist
touches the client to provide a corrective experience, the therapist's touch conveys her authentic feelings. If it is tentative or per-
functory, the client will probably know. Because of the client's
increased sensitivity in this state, the client will be much more at-
tuned to a therapist's fears and to inauthentic caring communicated by touch. What Carl Rogers called *unconditional positive
regard* is very important in a nonordinary state session. His Client
Centered Therapy expresses unconditional positive regard through
presence and verbal response with clients in ordinary states of
consciousness. When the client is in an age-regressed or transpersonal state of nonordinary consciousness, often with eyes closed,
we can often express unconditional positive regard and compassion more efficiently and directly by presence and touch, than by
talking.

Integrating profound experiences

Safety includes both preparing clients to enter the nonordinary state and preparing them for the return to ordinary consciousness and daily life. Because the nonordinary and ordinary worlds
feel so different, the transition can be more difficult if clients are
not prepared.

How do we, as therapists or facilitators, prepare clients to integrate these experiences which may be viewed as extreme and
incredible by most of their culture? Modern culture is deeply invested in ordinary reality, in the dichotomy of truth and lie, cause
and effect, and good and bad. One of our jobs as caregivers work-

ing with nonordinary states is to affirm the other, nonordinary reality our clients have experienced and at the same time prepare clients for the rejection of that reality by their social system. This is as true for experiences with "spiritual" and transpersonal content as with child abuse and other trauma. Those who are invested in ordinary consciousness are often frightened by the phenomena of nonordinary states which threaten their denial or belief systems. Therapists who feel threatened may react to their client with rejection or punitive action.

When a therapist helps a client establish a certain vulnerability during a nonordinary state experience, the therapist has a parallel responsibility to help the client manage the transition back to ordinary reality. Having shown a client how to open the door to non-ordinary reality, the therapist may be ethically bound to assist the client in learning how to close that door at the end of the session.

The therapist can talk to the client about how to speak with others about his nonordinary experiences. After discussing how the client can decide with whom he wants to share his experience, the therapist can suggest that the client share slowly, gauging how much someone really wants to know about his experience.

He can also talk in general terms. Perhaps the client had a past-life experience in which he felt he was an Inquisitor in the Spanish Inquisition and felt the similarity between that role and the pain and rage his own childhood perpetrator must have felt while torturing him. If this client described the scene and these feelings and added how re-experiencing such horror had helped him integrate a piece of his own abuse history, he would deliver a huge emotional load to the listener. His listener may have casually asked, *What happened in therapy today?* or *What happened in the workshop you went to last weekend?* In this situation, the therapist might recommend the client begin sharing by saying that he had an important experience that helped him understand some of his life. If the listener is still interested, he might go on to say that it involved his abuse history or it involved feeling intense emotions.

Probably, only a few people will be interested in and able to understand all the details and the full impact of the experience.

The therapist can talk to the client about how to treat himself with care and kindness in the time immediately following the session. The therapist can, for example, suggest hot baths, vitamin C, lots of fluids to drink, and that the client take time to rest, find quiet solitude, and do journal writing or drawing to integrate his experiences in nonordinary reality with his ordinary life.

The therapist also has a responsibility to see that the client is safely back into ordinary, automobile-driving consciousness at the close of a session. The therapist should schedule and time nonordinary sessions so that there is some flexibility in allowing for the return to consciousness. Usually such work takes longer than the 50-minute hour—one and a half to two hours or more is more realistic. Herman describes Kluft's (1989) "rule of thirds" in which abreactive work in trauma recovery happens within a session divided into thirds. This pattern of working is useful for other nonordinary state work as well. Kluft structures the session so that the nonordinary state work begins in the first third, comes to intensity and finishes in the second third. In the final third of the session, the therapist gives the client time to reorient himself and return to ordinary functioning.[74]

Cognitive dissonance

The potential for cognitive dissonance is greater in nonordinary state work. Cognitive dissonance, in turn, makes the potential for somatic/psychospiritual crisis greater. Knowledge and understanding gained in the nonordinary state may create cognitive dissonance with the values and habits of the client in the ordinary consciousness of daily life. The client may find it difficult to tolerate the clash of apparently opposing constructs.

For example, the sudden understanding that she was abused may confront her cherished belief that she had a happy childhood. The belief in a loving God may be hard to integrate with an overwhelming encounter with the pain and suffering of life. Perhaps the client finds that some comfortably familiar categories of happiness and pain, right and wrong, or joy and suffering no longer adequately define a new, more complex understanding.

If the client is unable to tolerate these conflicts, she may become nonfunctional in ordinary life while she processes these paradoxes. The conflict might demonstrate itself somatically, psychologically, or spiritually. The ability to tolerate paradox is a razor's edge of spiritual development. The Zen koan is an attempt to jam the mind with paradox or riddle so that consciousness transcends the smaller paradigm of the mind. Nonordinary state experiences challenge the limited belief system of the ordinary state, and thus, serve the same function. There are various therapeutic ways to help a client stretch with the paradox without breaking.

Somatic or psychospiritual crisis

When a client does not have a good self-observing ego or a history of satisfactory functioning in ordinary life, she may not be a good candidate for nonordinary state work. If she is already experiencing a great degree of cognitive dissonance or is working with nonordinary states of consciousness, whether it is a weekend sweat lodge or a half hour of EMDR, she may more likely be overwhelmed by additional nonordinary state work. It is always a good idea to assess with a client before a session whether nonordinary state work is appropriate and well-timed.

Is there an overload of stress in the client's ordinary life already? Does she seem excited to participate or is she reluctant to engage in experiential, nonordinary therapeutic work at this time? Does she have a supportive network of friends and family to provide a safety net if she becomes disoriented for a short period of time? Has she shown some flexibility in entering brief states of nonordinary consciousness (*e.g.,* guided meditation) and returning easily to ordinary functioning?

Occasionally, even if well-timed, sessions in nonordinary states will initiate a transformative, somatic, psychospiritual crisis (spiritual emergency) in a quite unexpected way. Some people do not make their transformations in small steps, but in dramatic leaps.

Does the client have an overload of stress in her ordinary life? On occasion, a quiet meditation, a guided imagery sequence, or a breathwork session will be just the key to create this kind of opening. To provide an extra measure of safety, the therapist and client together could have a plan of action, including supportive in-patient referrals ready in the relatively rare event of a crisis.

Assessing Client Readiness for Nonordinary State Work

■ Is the client eager to participate?

■ Does the client have supportive family and friends?

■ Has the client shown ability to flexibly enter nonordinary states and re-enter ordinary states?

■ Is the client stressed, over-tired, or overwhelmed at present?

Client's needs for nurturing, sexual contact, and spiritual connection

A client in a nonordinary state often has strong needs for nurturing, sexual contact, and spiritual connection.[75] The potential for transference is greater because of these personal desires and spiritual longings. In addition to biographical transference in which the client sees the therapist as her mother, father, or lover, the client can transpose onto the therapist various archetypal images and qualities ranging from divine and godlike to demonic. The powerful energies present in a nonordinary state can precipitate anything from con-fusion in the therapeutic relationship to persistent client attempts at seduction and boundary violations. A client can feel devotion to or paranoia about the therapist well beyond what is normally found in ordinary state therapy sessions.

Very strong transferences develop quickly in the hypnotized person adding to the moral responsibility not to exploit the client's tendency to obedience. Caregiver abuses of client transference can include coercion, sexual seduction, or influencing the client to perform some behavior or act which she would not have done otherwise.[76]

Subtle and compelling countertransference issues

Much has been written about the client's need to learn or rebuild basic physical, emotional, and spiritual trust through the therapeutic relationship. The vulnerability of the person in a nonordinary state should invoke a high code of honor in the caregiver. It is incumbent on the therapist to recognize and work effectively with both transference and countertransference.

Countertransference can include feelings of skepticism, guilt, hate, contempt, disgust, sadism, voyeurism, arousal, jealousy, envy, as well as extremes of sympathy, love, solicitousness, and wanting to be the extraordinary, all-knowing healer. It can also encompass situations where the caregiver can physically feel a client's body sensations and symptoms or link intuitively with the client through dreaming and extra-sensory perception.[77]

While a certain degree of conscious diffusion of boundaries and countertransference is very helpful in understanding what is going on with the client, nonordinary states may make it more difficult for the therapist to know when he has crossed the line into the area of true enmeshment, codependence, and ultimately client harm. Nonordinary states also produce an aura of "specialness" about the quality of therapeutic work together, which obfuscates boundaries that might be quite clear and easily honored in work with clients in ordinary states of consciousness.

Money, Sex, and Power

Work with clients in nonordinary states does not mean we need a whole new ethical code. The old ethical principles having to do with money, sex, and power are just as important to continue to apply when clients are in nonordinary states. It may be helpful in these times to approach the old issues of money, sex, and power with an expanded awareness, an increasing sensitivity to these well known issues arising in ways we have not considered, and to add an expanded list of new issues that particularly apply to working with clients in nonordinary states of consciousness.

Most ethical issues in ordinary therapy with clients concern money, sex, and power. Although most professional codes of ethics do not use the headings money, sex, and power to list their guidelines, most of the ethical principles listed concern these areas. Professional peer review of ethical misconduct almost always regards one or more of these issues. Below are some of the behaviors commonly considered unethical by therapeutic professions.

Money, sex, and power seem to have a *lower octave* and a *higher octave*. In what I am calling the lower octave, the issues are clearer. They concern tangible reality, recognizable behavior, and factual data. An ethical violation or an issue of transference or countertransference is usually fairly blatant to someone who knows professional ethical codes or who understands psychological dynamics. Therapists who act unethically are commonly motivated by personal desires or personal fears. For example, they want more money (personal desire or greed), and so keep a client in treatment when she is no longer benefiting. Therapists might also worry (personal fear) that they cannot pay their bills this month which might persuade them to falsify insurance forms to collect more money in fees.

In the higher octaves of money, sex, and power issues, landmarks are more scarce. Spiritual longings and fears get mixed up with the personal desires and fears in a confusing package. For example, the personal desire for sex becomes the spiritual longing for mystical sex and spiritual union. When money, sex, and power issues take on a transpersonal flavor, they have the compelling nature of a spiritual or inner call that is quite bewildering.

Some Unethical Money Behaviors

■ **Retaining a client who is not benefiting from therapy in order to keep receiving the fee**

■ **Accepting payment for a referral**

■ **Charging excessive fees**

■ **Not disclosing the fee structure**

■ **Borrowing money from a client**

The caregiver may believe he is the one to embody the spiritual aspirations of his client through sex, and vice versa. This is a powerful example of countertransference because ordinary reality and nonordinary reality (myth and spiritual energies) are entangled. The spiritual development part seems *good*. The sexual fantasies seem *good*. The nonordinary state relationship seems *good*. The caregiver knows that misuse of sex and power are *bad*, but he does not want to believe that spiritual sex is misuse of power.

Some Unethical Sexual Behaviors

■ Physical sexual contact

■ Sexual harassment

■ Responding to client's romantic fantasies in a way which leads the client to believe infatuation is mutual and may become a relationship outside of therapy.

Peter Rutter in his book, *Sex in the Forbidden Zone,* writes of male therapists: "When intoxicated by their sexual fantasies, they can easily develop magical feelings of power and invulnerability that cloud their judgment. . . .He feels either that he is untouchable by the outside world or that the sexual relationship he is seeking is so important that it is worth any risk."[78]

Some Unethical Power Behaviors

■ Inappropriately influencing a client's decisions or actions, such as which spiritual path to follow

■ Using clients to further one's own interests

■ Disclosing client confidences

■ Hiding behind transference (*e.g.,* claiming the role of Healer)

When disciplinary actions are brought against caregivers for their spiritual/sexual connection with clients, even then they may feel they did nothing wrong. The disciplinary action might seem *unfair* to them. *Good* and *bad, fair* and *unfair* as concepts themselves can become quite perplexing.

Most of the cases of sexual misconduct involving nonordinary states which have come to my attention surprised me. I think the therapists involved were surprised by their own actions as well. These were therapists who felt they would never succumb to a physical lust with a client but found themselves unexpectedly vulnerable to spiritual lust. Their personal desires and fears were mixed with spiritual longings and spiritual fears. Rutter explains this in his book: "The act of intercourse can allow us to experience in the most intense way possible our deepest biological, emotional, and spiritual strivings. . . . The erotic energy in our fantasies can also serve as a medium of expression for our deepest nonsexual aspirations."[79]

To the three major personal issues of money, sex, and power, I have added four other areas. These are areas where therapists working with clients in nonordinary states and with transpersonal issues can encounter ethical pitfalls related to a mixture of personal desires, fears, and spiritual longings. I call the four additional areas: love, truth, insight, and oneness. The following chapters discuss each of these seven areas.

4

A Model for Examining Our Vulnerabilities

This model incorporates the paradoxical truths that
spiritual (and ethical) growth
involve practice and developmental work,
yet, at the same time,
grace or liberation from suffering
is always instantaneously available.

—K.T.

$\mathcal{I}$ have designed a model which describes the ethical issues pertaining to work with clients and the vulnerabilities caregivers have to ethical misconduct when clients have profound and intense experiences. This model may be helpful for those of us who wish to examine our own countertransference in therapy situations, especially those involving nonordinary states of consciousness and transpersonal issues.

One basis for this model is the map of the chakras taken from kundalini yoga and Hinduism. Another part is taken from Buddhism. Other concepts, common to the teachings of many great religions, are taken loosely from their original scriptures in order to create a working model for the purposes of this book. This model incorporates the paradoxical truths that spiritual (and ethical) growth involves practice and developmental work, yet, at the same time, grace or liberation from suffering is always instantaneously available.

The model for examining our ethical issues, however, is not meant to be religious in any way—neither traditionally nor radically. Rather, I have constructed a model with a familiar form which can contain and let us view the ways in which ethical issues arise in therapeutic situations.

The model and its metaphors

According to yogic scriptures, the human body has a number of subtle energy centers (seven, traditionally) called *chakras*. These centers correspond to the physical nerve plexes in the body. A central energy channel called the *shushumna*, whose corresponding physical location is the spine, threads together these subtle energy centers. This system describes the evolutionary life force of the human body as lying dormant at the base of the spine. In Sanskrit the evolutionary life force is called *kundalini*.

When the kundalini awakens, it begins its journey up the shushumna and through the major chakras. Kundalini Shakti is a metaphor for the principle of manifest consciousness (*i.e.,* matter and energy). Shakti moves upward from its denser, lower center manifestations and transforms its energy into a different form or expression at each center. At last, the refined and transformed consciousness of Shakti merges with Shiva at the crown or seventh center. Shiva is the metaphor for the principle of unmanifest consciousness (the concept of the void from which all manifests). The union of Shiva and Shakti symbolizes the unity of all energy and consciousness.

This movement of the kundalini is a process of physical and emotional cleansing and spiritual development coincident with transformation. As the kundalini becomes active and moves within the centers, the person encounters new abilities and challenges. The journey of the kundalini through the centers is not always linear—moving from the first to the second to the third, and so forth; sometimes the energy is active in one center, sometimes in another. In this model for examining our ethical issues, the issues of several centers may be active in any given therapeutic relationship, without regard to linearity.

The concept of right relationship

Buddhism teaches that we achieve freedom from suffering by letting go of our attachments to fears and desires. *The Noble Eightfold Path* counsels (1) Right Understanding; (2) Right Thought; (3) Right Speech; (4) Right Action; (5) Right Livelihood; (6) Right Effort; (7) Right Mindfulness; and (8) Right Concentration.[80] The word *Right* is not quite the correct word in English for this concept. *Right*, as it is used here, connotes appropriateness, love, and truthfulness, rather than perfection or the opposite of some arbitrary "wrong."

I gather all of these aspects into one concept of *right relationship* and use the shushumna as the straight line depicting right relationship. Right relationship honors the integrity of all parties involved and supports their well-being and spiritual growth. I use the shushumna, the central channel through the centers, as the right relationship track. (See *Caregiver Vulnerabilities to Ethical Misconduct* chart.) The straight line is symbolic of our clear therapeutic intention to care and to do a good job. The shushumna illustrates right relationship to spirit in that the line is straight and connected between matter and consciousness. It describes the most conscious expression of human energy in all its various forms. When the line is straight, neither the caregiver nor the client is distracted from therapeutic and developmental intention by the force of fears, desires, or longings along the way. The straight line of the shushumna also symbolizes right relationship of the caregiver and client to each other in the therapeutic relationship. In right relationship we intend to move through our own issues to wholeness and to shepherd the spiritual emergence energy of a client along its natural develop-mental track. Another way to express this is through the Christian term *stewardship*. The right relationship track is also the path of Christian stewardship of energy and resources. Stewardship implies conscious and appropriate caretaking.

Human energy moves from the first center toward its goal of uniting with spirit in the seventh. In the yogic metaphor, Shakti (matter and energy) is moving toward *right relationship* to Shiva (spirit) by manifesting and mastering every form of human energy (represented by the centers). Each center has certain characteristics and when our human/spiritual energy is operating in each it takes a different form. Human/spiritual energy in the sex center expresses itself as sexual energy. Human/spiritual energy in the power center expresses itself as empowerment. Each center changes the form and the issues encountered by the energy that moves through it. In this model, I have named the seven centers: money, sex, power, love, truth, insight, and oneness to correspond with what is generally agreed upon to be the character of each of the centers.[81]

Christian traditions have contributed some of this model's *keys to professional ethical behavior* (See *Chapter 13*) that keep us on the path of right relationship. Christian contributions including authentic caring (do unto others as you would have them do unto you[82]) and willingness to examine our own motivations (looking not for the mote in another's eye, but looking first for the beam in our own eye[83]). Many other religions contribute a spiritual precept of humility (willingness to ask for help and learn) and truth (authenticity).

This model of *Caregiver Vulnerabilities to Ethical Misconduct* provides a general map of the somatic/psychospiritual journey and points out potholes and distractions that might show up along the road. It may help in conceptualizing this model to think

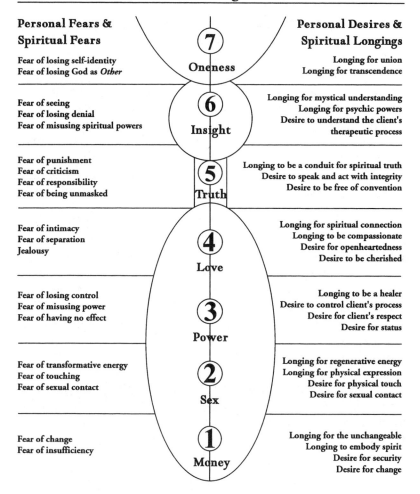

Personal Fears &
Spiritual Fears

Personal Desires &
Spiritual Longings

Fear of losing self-identity
Fear of losing God as *Other*

Longing for union
Longing for transcendence

⑦ Oneness

Fear of seeing
Fear of losing denial
Fear of misusing spiritual powers

Longing for mystical understanding
Longing for psychic powers
Desire to understand the client's
therapeutic process

⑥ Insight

Fear of punishment
Fear of criticism
Fear of responsibility
Fear of being unmasked

Longing to be a conduit for spiritual truth
Desire to speak and act with integrity
Desire to be free of convention

⑤ Truth

Fear of intimacy
Fear of separation
Jealousy

Longing for spiritual connection
Longing to be compassionate
Desire for openheartedness
Desire to be cherished

④ Love

Fear of losing control
Fear of misusing power
Fear of having no effect

Longing to be a healer
Desire to control client's process
Desire for client's respect
Desire for status

③ Power

Fear of transformative energy
Fear of touching
Fear of sexual contact

Longing for regenerative energy
Longing for physical expression
Desire for physical touch
Desire for sexual contact

② Sex

Fear of change
Fear of insufficiency

Longing for the unchangeable
Longing to embody spirit
Desire for security
Desire for change

① Money

Caregiver Vulnerabilities to Ethical Misconduct

of the shushumna of right relationship as a rubber band stretched vertically. The fears, desires, and spiritual longings pertaining to each center wait along the sidelines. Each center has its own special vulnerabilities to attachment through desire or longing and through fear. A situation involving ethics usually involves more than one center's issues. The rubber band can be pulled to one side or the other. The resulting zigzag course makes the flow of energy and clear communication more difficult. Identifying the issue, on the other hand, often allows us some objectivity and detachment. Knowing where we are off track helps us reorient and straighten the path toward the right relationship we wanted at the beginning of the caregiving relationship.

If a caregiver should find himself shoulder deep in one of these potholes, he can stick out his head and take a look at the seven center model. Hopefully, this will help him pinpoint which fear, desire, or spiritual longing has attracted him, causing him to steer off course. Subsequently, each of the centers has its own chapter. Each chapter includes suggestions to help the caregiver begin the search for appropriate use of the energies of that center. Each caregiver's situation is unique so each of the chapters has questions to facilitate self-reflection.

This model expands the possibilities for ethical consciousness by naming the issues of each center. These issues apply not only to ordinary states and traditional therapy, but also to nonordinary states and transpersonal therapy, bodywork, and spiritual counsel. They apply particularly to those profound moments in any truly healing therapeutic relationship. In an ethical helping relationship, the caregiver allows the client's energy to work out its own issues in various arenas. The caregiver supports the client but is careful not to let his own fears, desires, or spiritual longings distort the client's process.

I believe that almost everyone who works with clients in or out of nonordinary states wants to do a good job. We care about our clients. We want them to achieve healing, insight, and their desired behavioral changes, and to have a positive outcome to their experience with nonordinary states. We begin a therapeutic relationship wanting to be in right relationship. Usually, we welcome help in staying in right relationship to our clients.

In the following chapters, I discuss each center and its issues one by one, giving some examples of the issues a therapist, minister, or practitioner might have in working with a client. I talk about these issues under the headings of countertransference (the spiritual longings, personal desires, and fears of the caregiver) and transference (the spiritual longings, personal desires, and fears of the client). In each chapter I give some suggestions for how to use the energies of each center in a therapeutic context and prevent distraction from the therapeutic intention.

Each of the seven chapters has a suggested list of questions for self-reflection. The caregiver may have a sense that the therapeutic relationship is off track—somewhere between nonproductive and harmful—but be mystified as to where it veered off course. The questions near the end of each chapter may be a way to begin the caregiver's self-examination process.

5

Money

Money—The first center

Change underlies the issues of the first center. Change, exchange (money), and security are also primary issues in this center. I have chosen to call this center "money" only because many unethical actions seem to involve money as the symbol for change, exchange, and security.

The issue of security implies change and the love/hate relationship we have with change. We want change, yet we fear change at the same time. Changes means giving up the old and known for the new and unknown. Spiritual transformation is change.

Christina Grof wrote, "My entire being aspired toward something I could not identify. . . . The "thirst of our soul for wholeness . . . the union with God," as Jung called it, is a fundamental impetus within us that has great power in our lives. The drive to know our true selves elicits a kind of divine discontent within.[84] We want spiritual development, yet we fear it simultaneously because we know that change means loss of one thing in order to have the new.

It is easy to forget that spiritual longing begins symbolically in the first center. It is the place where we, who apparently have been separated from Spirit, wake up and begin our conscious longing to realize our oneness with the unchangeable. It is where we begin to acknowledge that we want to embody Spirit. We want to realize our own identity with that which is eternal.

Countertransference—Spiritual longings and fears related to money, change, and security

When a client awakens and begins his spiritual journey, a caregiver may remember her own spiritual longings.

As caregivers we may have different responses to a client's awakening. We may be inspired to deepen our own spiritual practice. We may want to encourage the client to do spiritual development in the same ways we did it or in ways we think we should have done it. Paradoxically, the part of caregivers which is matter-oriented resists both these responses and simply feels insecure. That part of us feels the fear of change itself. It wants security and desires things to continue always as they are now. That part of us intuits that change and transformation imply loss.

A caregiver may be afraid of his client's spiritual progress. He may fear that the changes he is seeing in her will force him to have a different perception of spiritual matters or psychological ones. The spiritual and psychological may interact in new ways that threaten his working model of the human psyche.

A therapist or spiritual counselor may compare his spiritual progress to his client's and experience jealousy. The client is having tangible effects pointing to spiritual change. Her body may be moving spontaneously, she may be having visions, or her meditation practice may be effortless and meditation itself prolonged. The therapist, too, longs to have such results.

Countertransference—Personal desires and fears related to money, change, and security

Money is the metaphor for the issues of physical, mental, emotional, and spiritual survival or security. This center concerns personal fears of material insufficiency. The fear of insufficiency creates a desire for anything the client has to offer which seems to satisfy that anxiety. The therapist wants to keep a paying client even when he should refer or terminate therapy. The therapist wants to keep a gift the client offers. The therapist wants to accept a favor such as a loan to build a new therapy center.

In the first center, there is an undercurrent of neediness. The therapist may need the client to provide compliments and bolster insufficient self-esteem. The therapist may want the client to help her find contacts for other financial opportunities, such as teaching and consulting. The therapist may want the client to refer other clients to her. The therapist may be interested in negotiating an attractive barter situation in exchange for therapy or to receive free professional advice from someone (*e.g.,* a doctor or lawyer) who is in therapy with her. All these needs imply insufficiency. In any of these hypothetical cases, the therapist feels she does not have either enough money or enough ability to get the things she needs outside of her therapeutic relationships with clients.

Caregivers may feel personal fears of insufficiency (*I am not a good enough therapist)* or insufficiency as spiritual practitioners (*I have not been meditating long enough to know how to help her*). The caregiver may feel in awe of the client's process or spiritual abilities in such a way that he compares his own progress or spiritual abilities unfavorably. *I haven't had a kundalini awaken-*

ing yet. He may then depend upon the client for reassurance and compliments in order to bolster his self-esteem.

Transference related to money, change, and security

Parents may help determine the child's relationship to God. If the child loves and trusts them, he may more easily imagine a trustworthy, loving God. In the same way, the therapist can, in reparenting, find herself the repository of the client's transitional and developmental trust. This development of trust ultimately can carry over to the client's relationship to God, Spirit, or his Higher Power. The therapist's trustworthiness and her ability to be in right relationship in the first center will allow the client to begin to feel a spiritual security through which he can deepen his process.

The client may identify the therapist as the cause of change (and therefore loss) or the cause of his difficult or blessed spiritual opening. He may blame or attribute strong spiritual powers to the therapist. This situation would also bring up issues connected with the third center (see *Chapter 7*). In the first example, the client attributes all the blame for the client's process to the therapist. In the second example the therapist is given all the credit for the healing.

- *You are to blame for making me remember my awful childhood! If you hadn't used hypnosis, I would never have gone through all this pain.*

- *You are the one who has retrieved parts of my soul for me. Now I feel whole and healed. It is all because of you!*

Using the energy of money, change, and security appropriately

Therapy in ordinary states of consciousness is about change. Therapy in nonordinary states can sometimes mean radical and rapid change. Psychospiritual crisis and transformation may affect income, sexual desire, and aggressive impulses and increase the need for therapeutic or supportive services. When things are changing quickly for the client in many areas, the clear, stable therapeutic contract is more important. The client has more than the usual need for clarity about fees, sexual boundaries, non-violence, techniques to be used, confidentiality, time and place, and the availability of the caregiver.

Strong therapeutic agreements about the process and ground rules (meta-agreements) provide meta-security (security about the security agreements) for both caregiver and client. (See *Chapter 3*.) This meta-security provides some protection while a client is giving up psychic security to face change itself. The client may also lose some of her physical security if she has changes in employment, relationship, or geographic location.

Ironically, surrender to change is a prerequisite to mastery of material, emotional, and spiritual life. The caregiver conveys to her client her own willingness to trust and surrender. Unfortunately, she usually conveys whatever fears she has in these areas as well. A caregiver's own inexperience with moving through a particular issue may block a client's progress. A caregiver will find it hard to go anywhere with a client where she has not traveled himself. Stanislav Grof writes: "Unless the therapist deals successfully with these issues: fear of death, total loss of control, [and the] specter of insanity, the manifestations of the deep unconscious of the client will tend to activate his or her own problem areas and trigger difficult emotional and psychosomatic responses."[85]

The caregiver can pay close attention to the safety needs of the client. She can make clear agreements and keep them. She can communicate her own trust in the inner process that is beginning to unfold in the client and encourage the client to trust and surrender to the change that is beginning to happen.

If the caregiver feels neediness herself, it may be a mental reaction to the emotion of fear. She may be defending herself from her own fears of insufficiency. It may also be a clue that the client has repressed fear in this area.

The caregiver can affirm the beginning of a major transformative process in the client's life and give him information about similar processes of others by referring him to literature and other resources.[86] The caregiver can assist the client in staying focused on his inner development rather than displacing his fear of change and desire for security onto his external environment, including the caregiver.

Self-reflection related to money, change, and security

- Do I fear change in general? In this specific case?

- What are my next steps on my own psychospiritual path at this time? What are my specific resistances to taking these next steps?

- Have I admitted to myself that I have spiritual longings?

- Can I recommit to habits and practices which will take me further toward my spiritual, therapeutic, or developmental goals without involving the client?

- Do I feel insufficient with regard to money?

- Do I feel insufficient with regard to my professional competence? If so, in what ways?

- Do I feel insufficient in my own spiritual "achievements"? If so, how?

- Are there any ways in which I have been, either unconsciously or consciously, using a client for financial gain, to try to feel more secure, or to acquire more self-esteem?

Cross-referencing money, change, and security issues with issues in the other centers

In some sense the issues of change and insecurity may thread their way through the issues addressed in any of the centers. (See *Chapters 6* through *11*.) The client's fear of change in any therapeutic situation and the caregiver's fear of her own or her client's transformation can play a role in any of these issues. Likewise the longing for the unchangeable is the force that propels transformation itself and moves a process through difficult issues at each center.

Money as an issue is not usually related to the other centers, except as it pertains to the third center, power. (See *Chapter 7*.) Insufficiency, however, often relates to the other centers, lending a quality of scarcity to each characteristic (*e.g.,* insufficient sexual drive or ability, insufficient mastery or power, insufficient compassion, and lack of ability to know or tell the truth, have insight, or attain spiritual union.)

6

Sex

*If the relationship is lived out sexually it becomes
no longer only the vessel in which the healing process
takes place, it becomes an end in itself
and thus destroys the therapy.*[87]

—Adolf Guggenbühl-Craig

Sex—The second center

Sexual energy is spiritual energy. When spiritual energy begins working in the psychophysical center called sex (the second
center), it takes the form of sensual feelings, sexual sensations,
evocative thoughts, deep emotions, and bodily expression. Spirit is
moving in the body and the body has sensations. When this energy
moves from another center into the second center, the hu-

man/spiritual energy does not change its essential nature, but its form does change.

The energy in this center is regenerative and transformative. All of us want more energy and long for more life force. People who have energy moving in this center have an expanded life force, a libido that seems unlimited. These people are attractive. They are magnetic and charismatic. Something about them communicates that there is more to life than just matter, that human beings are infused with spirit. They communicate a hopefulness, an ebullience that others long to feel.

Countertransference—Spiritual longings and fears related to sex

Caregivers may long for their own experience of spiritual sexuality. Clients whose energy is in the second center may express their life energy in what appears to be a sexual (physical) way, but the spiritual part of it is foremost. They radiate life force and the mystery of that life force.

Mere physical libido is not nearly as attractive. Lust is more connected to personal desire and the attempt to satisfy that personal desire. The kind of spiritual sexuality I am referring to here is part of a transformational and transpersonal process. It is a longing for union that takes one beyond the personal, separate identity. It is surrender to the spontaneous, powerful, regenerative forces both within us and without us. A caregiver watching such a process in a client may long to feel it in herself also. She may be tempted to try to acquire it by having sex with the client who is in touch with this energy.

Caregivers also may long to feel the spiritual quality of a client's sexuality directed at themselves. A caregiver can feel the quality of reverence in this energy. Caregivers may have a conscious or unconscious wish to acknowledge the divine within them. If a client is acknowledging their divine nature for them, it is hard to resist.

Clients who are in a process involving the second center often use their bodies as if they were holy objects. They use their bodies to worship. They feel intensely the glorious gift of the sensuality of life. They spontaneously worship (usually without calling it worship) both the force that is emerging within them and the physical bodies of others they connect with in the process of such expressions of devotion. The opportunity to participate in such worship may be all but irresistible.

In addition to deep spiritual longings, caregivers may have deep spiritual fears of this powerful, transformative energy. The caregiver may feel he has a tiger by the tail. This transformative energy rests in latency in the first center. In the second center, it is more awakened. If that awakening becomes too frightening, the client *depresses* it and exhibits features of clinical depression. Clients may feel frightened and depressed, and the therapist may feel this way too. The therapist may unconsciously try to put the lid on the client's evolutionary life force because it is frightening. A therapist writes:

■ *Seven years ago, I had a client who was having a spiritual emergency. She was functional in her life but was having visions of demons during periodic nonordinary states of consciousness. Her visions reminded me of my own sexual abuse history that, at the time, I was unwilling to face. I suggested strongly that she take antipsychotic medication. I was somewhat, though not totally aware that I was making the suggestion for my own benefit. If she had started antipsychotics inappropriately, she might have aborted her own transformative process and risked tardive dyskinesia with long term use. Fortunately she left treatment with me and found someone else who could see her through her process. I have learned to be more sensitive to, acknowledge, and seek therapy for any of my own fears which are triggered by clients.*

Perhaps the client is expressing profound emotions of anger and grief that are difficult for the therapist. For example:

■ *If my client were really to express her anger, I might become frightened. I would like to emphasize "channeling" it "constructively," rather than just letting her express it during her therapy hour.*

■ *My client is grieving her human condition which includes the mystery of being and the mystery of disappearing into death. The grief becomes a passionate wail that touches to the core of my own unresolved existential sadness. In an attempt to relieve myself, I attempt to "fix" her, to comfort her with scripture or philosophy, instead of allowing her to feel this very real pain that pains me!*

Grief and anger are painful emotions to feel, but sometimes joy and ecstasy are also very difficult feelings to tolerate. When a therapist sees these emotions in a client, the all too apparent distance between his own rather flat emotional state and the client's vibrancy may trigger both spiritual longing and fear of insufficiency.

Countertransference—Personal desires and fears related to sex

When the energy begins moving in this second center, clients often become very sexual. They become spontaneously seductive, but not in the usual game-playing way. Caregivers may feel irresistibly attracted because of their own spiritual longings, as I have written above, or because of physical desires.

Clients share their vivid sexual dreams and fantasies. The person in a second center process may have visual images of sexual organs. These images may for a time become fairly constant. The client may experience sexual sensations which keep him intensely aroused for lengthy periods or in an ongoing way. Yogis and mystics have written about periods of spiritual practice in which they experience almost continuous arousal. Perhaps the self-flagellation by monks in the Middle Ages was partially to subdue a natural phenomenon in spiritual practice which they took to be the lust of the flesh. A woman I know had ongoing fantasies and dreams of sexual organs. For those who are not familiar with the sexual and physical manifestations of spiritual development, these phenomena may seem perverse or at least strange.

If these sexual phenomena occur for a client, a caregiver's tendency may be to find some external reason (some person to whom the client is attracted) for such unmitigated arousal. Not understanding the opening of second center energies, the caregiver's tendency may be to believe that the client is attracted to the caregiver.

Sex in general is problematic for us in this culture. Sex sells everything from blue jeans to automobiles, perhaps because we as a culture feel repressed and unfulfilled sexually. When the real thing—vital physical energy connected to its spiritual source— shows up in the office, a caregiver may be easily sold.

It is interesting that many television ads are now using spiritual images and concepts in combination with sexual ones to sell their products. Advertising agencies seem to have discovered the sales appeal of spiritual longings. They have also been skillful in mixing archetypal images which evoke spiritual longing with other images which appeal to sensuality or sexuality.

When the client is being openly provocative or simply sexually magnetic, the caregiver is often attracted and responsive. Sex is certainly the most prominent area of ethical violation. Most legal and ethical actions brought against caregivers are for infractions of laws and codes which prohibit sex between client and caregiver. (See *Chapter 14.*)

A caregiver may also encounter countertransference in the sex center from her own fear. She may see the client's sexuality spontaneously and powerfully unfolding and respond with a kind of psychic tightening of the therapeutic reins. The caregiver may fear the emergence of such uncontrolled, spontaneous sexual feeling in her own life. She may think that if she felt such energies she would not be able to channel them into ethical behavior. The caregiver may have moral judgments about the actions that the client is taking in response to the client's own sexualized, spiritual energy. If her client suddenly begins a passionate affair that threatens a long-term, secure marriage, the caregiver may not approve philosophically or theologically. The caregiver may even feel threatened in her own stable relationship by the power of sexual/spiritual passion to change priorities and ordinary circumstances.

Sexuality is often linked to anger and hostility. Grof discusses this connection in his description of the third stage of birth when the fetus experiences both aggression and sexual arousal.[88] If a client's process involves this combination it may be particularly difficult for the caregiver who has been harmed by abusive sexuality to remain objective.

Touch is an area which impacts both transference and countertransference. Opponents of therapist touch point out that therapists do not always know their own deepest motivations in responding to or initiating touch with a client. In touching the client unconsciously, they may be unwittingly taking the first step down the road to unethical behavior. (See also *Chapter 3*).

On the other hand, the therapist himself may fear physical touch. If he does, he may not be willing to touch the client when the client really needs a therapeutic, corrective touch. Because the therapist feels unclear about his own needs around touch, he will feel confused about whether or not touching is appropriate in any given situation. Fear of physical touch may keep therapists from appropriately touching a client who has regressed to infancy and who encounters the original trauma of not being touched and loved. If the therapist is unwilling to touch a client who is reliving such a trauma, the therapist is acting in a counter-therapeutic way—contributing to the re-enactment of trauma. *Not* touching the client in such a situation re-imprints the client's sense of unconditional *negative* regard or *untouchability* and may, at times, be unethical.

Conversely, if therapists have incorporated new age values of hugging and touching, they may feel as if they should *always* hug and touch a client, at least in response to a client's overture. They may neglect to follow their own intuition when it tells them hugging is not appropriate with certain clients or in certain situations.

If the therapist knows she has a deficit of touch in her own biography and, subsequently, a deep need to be touched, or a deep need to nurture, she also knows she may feel confused about appropriate touching in the context of therapy. As infants we all needed touch to thrive. Touch is important to older people and to sick people. Human beings seem to need and usually want physical touch. When a therapist encounters a person who is full of vital energy, the therapist may want to physically connect with that source of vitality. In touching a client, the therapist may be responding to her own need to contact the client's energy tangibly.

Transference related to sex

The client in a second center process may feel devotional. As I mentioned above, her spiritual longing is expressed as a longing for bodily union. She may idealize her caregiver as the divine lover. More accurately, she realistically sees the divine nature of certain people but tends not to see their human nature. There may be archetypal imagery involved in her fantasies. She may envision her caregiver as Shiva or Krishna. She may feel he is a great healer or teacher and that she wishes to serve him in any way he asks.

This kind of erotic imagery appears on temples in India and symbolizes both the esoteric union of matter and spirit, and the spiritual development possible through actual sexual union of two human beings. The ritual of tantric worship has provided a form to acknowledge and channel this kind of expression. Tantra, however, requires both a suitable, equal partner and the practitioner's self-discipline within a spiritual practice. In tantric ritual, after long training, the spiritual and physical potential of union can be contained and channeled. The energy of the sex center may elicit this kind of imagery as well as a fantasy that the caregiver is a tantric master or tantric partner waiting to teach or fulfill the client.

This powerful transference can cause havoc in a therapeutic relationship. It is difficult enough sometimes for a therapist to accept the transference role of mother, father, or other biographical character in the client's life. It can be quite a strain to a therapist's equanimity to accept and work with the transference of a client's own divine nature or of the image of god or goddess especially when the client's fantasy involves sexual devotion.

Therapeutically, clients can become confused by a caregiver's loving touch. Clients' interpretations of therapeutic touch will vary according to the type and degree of transference involved.

■ *One woman told of a confusing shift in the middle of her process. She was regressed and childlike in the session. The facilitator held her and nurtured her and suddenly she described herself as "flipping" into a very sexual place. She felt a lot of confusion, but she talked about it later with the facilitator and the session had a productive ending.*

Age regression and need for nurturing can be intertwined with sexual arousal in clients who have been sexually abused as children. Infantile needs and sexual arousal can be entangled when a client is experiencing a COEX combining elements of post-natal biography and birth. Such mixtures may be quite troubling to both client and caregiver. They can also provide opportunities for corrective healing if the caregiver can remain accepting and nurturing without reacting in fear to the client's sexual feelings or responding in a sexual way to the client's arousal.

It may be difficult to determine in advance what the client's transference might be and how the client might respond to touch. In the above examples, nurturing and sexuality were confusingly interrelated. In other cases, the client may feel the caregiver's touch is insensitive and without empathy, especially if that is the way she has experienced touch in the past. It may even feel patronizing or violating to the client. If the client's interpretation of caregiver touch is that the caregiver is sexually harassing, romantically misleading, or even indifferent, the caregiver may have a legal problem in addition to a therapeutic one.

Using the energy of sex appropriately

If the caregiver acts on his own attraction or the client's in an external way, it can divert the client's focus from the internal movement of the client's energy. The process, which is really an internal psychospiritual process, is subverted when the caregiver encourages sexual contact to fulfill his personal needs. The reasons for not having sex with a client are not essentially different in this case from those in any ordinary therapy. Clients who trust a healer or a spiritual teacher feel injured when that person puts his own needs ahead of his client's best interests.

Thus, the ethical codes and laws prohibiting sex between caregiver and client stand us in good stead at a time when the energy is not only sexual, but spiritual, and therefore even more compelling. While not preventing sexual misconduct, they are at least enough to give us pause and time for self-reflection before we act in a way that might cause harm.

When the client is in a nonordinary state of consciousness, the caregiver can encourage her to keep her eyes closed to stay focused on the internal process occurring. Prolonged eye contact between the caregiver and the client in a nonordinary state of consciousness often promotes confusing dissolution of boundaries and erotic transference and countertransference.[89] Readers may be familiar with the psychedelic phenomenon that can happen when someone who has taken a psychedelic drug looks at another person's face and sees that face transform into some projection from the hallucinator's unconscious. The other's countenance might turn into an image which substantiates an inner paranoia (such as a demon, or an enemy). The face might take on the appearance of a relative with whom there is unfinished business. Or, the face may change into a god for whom the client has devotion and deep longing.

This hallucinogenic quality of nonordinary states can be pronounced when someone has taken LSD. This effect can be also quite subtle in a hypnotic state or after a massage. In such circumstances the client may project, see, or sense intangible qualities, such as love or divine nature in the caregiver. The client may intuit that the caregiver and the client had a relationship in what she perceives as a past life. The client may then feel the therapeutic relationship is a reunion with the two parties taking up the same roles from their "past life."

The caregiver can use these projections therapeutically when the client has been adequately prepared for such transference and when there is minimal countertransference. Even when these conditions are met, the involvement of the sex center in nonordinary states makes the honorable therapeutic path more slippery. The hallucination which is so subtle that it is not perceived as an hallucination creates confusion between the inner and outer realities.

Group work can diffuse the power of such attachment and clarify the boundaries between nonordinary reality and ordinary reality. When the client shares his hallucination or fixation on the therapist in a therapeutic group setting or with a third person, others can help the client see the projection as coming from his own psyche. By talking about it openly, he can drain the fantasy of its power. He can more easily drop his fantasy that the relationship with the therapist is a romantic relationship or that it is an ordinary, nonprofessional relationship with the reciprocal expectations of a peer friendship.

■ *A woman who was participating in a series of nonordinary state sessions was overcome by a deep sexual attraction to someone who had been providing professional massage for her between sessions. Both client and therapist in this case had excellent*

*boundaries. The therapist listened, but did not con-
sider having a sexual relationship with his client. The
client shared with the group about her feelings despite her deep embarrassment. As her nonordinary
experiences continued she realized the connection
between her primal need for physical acceptance and
her attraction to this therapist who received her body
without judgment. Suddenly, with this insight, the
fantasies and the attraction disappeared.*

The one on one client session is a precarious place for
working out this kind of transference. It is more difficult to
have a good outcome when speaking about one's infatuation in
a private setting and speaking to the person with whom one is
enthralled. Pope and Bouhoutsos point out in their book, *Sexual Intimacy Between Therapists and Patients,* that a therapist is
not immune from reacting with deep personal pleasure when a client says that she finds him sexually attractive or that she is in love
with him. The therapist may take personally what is essentially
unrelated to the therapist as an individual. The transference may
be either biographical (related to the client's personal relationship
history) or archetypal (*e.g.,* projecting onto the therapist the divine
lover archetype). If there is mutual attraction, and the therapist
responds as if they had met under circumstances other than a professional relationship, it can be quite damaging to the client.[90] To
work with this situation appropriately, the therapist can examine
his own countertransference. He can point out the impersonal nature of transference to the client and help her investigate the sym-
bology of her specific transference.

Transference and touching

Touching can be appropriate and necessary in a therapeutic
relationship, especially as we have seen when the client is in regressed and other nonordinary states of consciousness. Appropriate use of the energy of this center may mean taking the risk to
offer decisive, loving touch.

■ *A congregation member has an ecstatic experience
during a church service, stands up, then falls back-
wards with body moving wildly. She needs the touch
of the minister and other members to feel safely
contained, to feel that her experience is accepted by
others, and to rest quietly for a period afterwards.*

Touch can also exacerbate transference or countertransference issues. If the client has requested touch in a verbal therapy
situation, the therapist can ask herself if touching is appropriate
with this client, in this situation, and at this time in therapy.

■ *Will withholding touch from this client be counter-
therapeutic at this time?*

■ *Are there clear sexual boundaries in this therapeutic
relationship?*

■ *Does the therapist believe that the client or his family
might misinterpret therapeutic touch as a sexual
overture?*

If the therapist has considered all these questions and decides
to touch the client, she then can monitor the client's response to
the touching carefully. She can watch the client's breathing pattern
to see if there comes a point at which the client is resisting or
holding. She can be alert for any sign of hesitancy and can discon-
tinue touching until the client asks again or until she re-negotiates
with her client what the situation requires.[91]

Therapists can investigate their own longings, desires, and
fears around the physical body, physical sex, spiritual sex, touch
and vital energy. Because the second center contains pitfalls which
are terribly dangerous therapeutically and professionally, therapists can seek out training and consultation as prevention. They
can certainly seek assistance at the first sign that their longings,
desires, or fears are triggered by a client's transformative process
in this center. Therapists can also examine their own current relationship to the transformative process of their own spiritual paths.

The caregiver who can acknowledge he is in the grip of erotic countertransference can provide himself with strong supervision. In this way he can not only avoid unethical behavior and legal crises, but actually use, if appropriate, the erotic countertransference to help his client develop a sense of sexual self. Mary Dale Sheller, a social worker, cites the work of Elizabeth Kassoff who lectures (1990) on the value of accepting erotic transference and countertransference, yet not acting on it sexually. Sheller says:

> *Kassoff would argue that when the sexual side of a client has been traumatized or never developed, a client can benefit through the knowledge that he or she is experienced as an emotional and sexual being by another. Therapy should be a safe place to learn this, because in therapy closeness and intimacy can exist and be valued without actual sexual contact.*[92]

In the Harvard Mental Health Newsletter in 1984, Kenneth S. Pope offers statistics from anonymous surveys that show almost 90% of therapists have been sexually attracted to a patient and more than half say they have been aroused during therapy. He advocates:

> *Graduate training, continuing education on programs, formal supervision, and . . . abandoning an unrealistic self-image. . . . to understand the nature and implications of these feelings and handle them in ways that do not harm patients.*[93]

Accepting erotic transference and acknowledging erotic countertransference may be difficult enough under ordinary circumstances in therapy. It is especially difficult when it is intertwined with spiritual devotion or shared transpersonal experiences. Consultation with someone who has had successful experience with this sort of therapeutic relationship is important. I do not make many unequivocal statements in this book, but I am about to make one: When spiritual longings and fears and nonordinary states of consciousness are involved in a client relationship in combination with erotic transference or countertransference, then the therapist, minister, practitioner, or caregiver will find that ongoing, competent consultation is essential to a successful therapeutic relationship and outcome.

Self reflection on sex

- Am I attracted to the client?

- Am I vulnerable to my client's adoration?

- Has the client requested touch or am I the one initiating touch?

- Do I have strong needs to give or receive nurturing touch?

- Am I afraid to give or receive touch?

- Do I believe I should *always* respond to a request for nurturing touch?

- If I am touching the client, am I monitoring her responses closely?

- Do I tend to want to hold back the transformative process, particularly if it has anything to do with sex?

- Does the next risk in my own psychospiritual journey have to do with touch or sex?

- Is touching the client in this case therapeutic or counter-therapeutic? Is not touching the client therapeutic or counter-therapeutic?

- Can I talk comfortably about my client's sexual feelings and fantasies and rejoice with her in her newly discovered sexuality or spiritual sexuality?

- Is my sexual energy depressed at the moment? Am I exhibiting features of clinical depression myself?

- Do I have moral judgments about my client's fantasies or sexual behavior?

- Am I encouraging my client to see her process as an internal one?

- Would it be useful to my client if I acknowledge to her that I am attracted to her, while maintaining certainty for both of us that I will not act out my attraction sexually?

- Have I been giving myself reasons why my normal ethical code of conduct should be set aside in this one particular case?

Cross-referencing sex issues with issues in the other centers

Ethical misconduct often involves sex. In many ethically troubling cases where there has been no actual sexual behavior, there have been romantic undertones and confusing double messages.

Sex is the way we are accustomed to achieve union. We are attracted to that which we are lacking in ourselves in order to feel complete. Therefore sex is often used as a way to unconsciously become one with what we want: money, power, love, truth, and insight. We might attempt to fill this need for wholeness through union with a client who displays one of these qualities. (See *Chapters 1,* and *3* through *10.*)

If someone is dealing with sex as the primary ethical issue, he might refer to the section on telling the truth to ourselves in *Chapter 13.* He might also want to read over the sections on underestimation of the power of nonordinary states of consciousness to affect us and unacknowledged longings for love and spiritual connection in *Chapter 12.*

7

ower

To see power as the ability to enhance others' lives
expands society's narrow understanding of
more traditional concepts of power.[94]

—Pythia S. Peay

Power—The third center

The third center symbolizes the longing to effect change and to master processes. It is the place where we integrate our fears, needs, desires, and spiritual longings with the means to obtain them. Because control is necessary for mastery, the third center also deals with issues of control. Power, mastery, and control can be in the service of enabling others to find their own empowerment. Power, mastery, and control can also become ends in themselves, to be achieved at the expense of others.

Countertransference—Spiritual longings and fears related to power

Therapists long to have the power to make a healing contribution to a client's life. Ministers and caregivers long to achieve the result of a better quality of life for those in their charge. As transpersonal therapists, they want to use their skills to increase consciousness and awareness. They want to help a client expand her frame of reference and to come to terms with existential issues using the client's own experiences to shape her beliefs and values. Spiritually aware caregivers have a deep longing to use any spiritual power they have with integrity and discrimination so that they can help those who seek assistance from them.

Caregivers may also encounter fear of spiritual power in the power center. They may waver back and forth. First they feel they are powerless and ineffectual.

■ *I cannot help my client. I am not a shaman. I cannot travel into the other worlds with her and protect her.*

Then they fear that they have too much power and that they may misuse it.

■ *I know what is going to happen next in my client's process. It is almost as if I am directing it and she is reading my mind to know what to do next.*

Countertransference—Personal desires and fears related to power

The longing to contribute and to achieve mastery is the higher octave (spiritual longing) of power. In the lower octave (personal desires and fears) of power, a person wants not only to contribute and to achieve mastery, but also to have an effect on the opinions of others. He wants others, peers and clients, to think of him as special and wonderful. He needs appreciation or acknowledgment to affirm his mastery.

Caregivers naturally desire the client's respect. If they are attached to getting it, however, they are controlled by their own need for a certain client attitude. In Transactional Analysis (TA), Eric Berne describes a dynamic called a *game* (a predictable pattern of dynamics between people) called *Gee, you're wonderful, professor!*[95] In this interaction the caregiver needs acclaim and status. She needs it so badly that she is willing to disempower the client (student) in order to get it. *I am wonderful*, the caregiver acquiesces, and you, the client, are not *as* wonderful, therefore your role is to tell me how wonderful I am. The position of unconditional wonderfulness for one party (the caregiver) and not for the other (the client) is spiritually unsound. Whenever a caregiver takes this position she tends to go off the track of right relationship in the power center, even if the client does not.

Energy in the power center is often forced off its track of service and mastery by a desire to control. Caregivers may feel they should know where the process is going. In nonordinary state work, they simply cannot know. They are unable to predict the direction of the process. Any attempt to do so may actually be counter-therapeutic. Anticipating and second-guessing may interfere with the natural direction taken by the client's inner healer.

One therapist told her supervisor, "I do not feel I am doing enough for this client." She gave her supervisor the details and he replied, "I think we underestimate the enormous value of just listening in the most tuned-in, empathic way we possibly can."[96]

When therapists are attached to outcome in nonordinary state work, they feel as if they are doing something wrong if something unforeseen happens in the client's process. If something unanticipated and *negative* occurs, the therapist may feel responsible and guilty. If the unexpected result feels *positive*, the therapist may feel inadequate for *not* causing it or for *not* expecting it. Alternately, therapists might deny the event surprised them and claim in subtle ways to have made it happen. All of these reactions are the result of attachment to power.

Therapists may want to be seen by the client as *doing* something to earn their money. They want the client's respect and the status of being a healer. They believe they earn that by accomplishing and doing. In the traditional therapeutic systems which are designed for working with clients in ordinary states of consciousness, we therapists were trained to know answers, execute strategies, and implement techniques. In making the transition to therapeutic work in nonordinary states, merely being present and trusting the process may not seem like doing adequate therapy. Simply creating a therapeutic context of expanded space to contain the unexpected event and the larger frame of reference may not feel powerful enough.

In so-called New Age therapies, *doing* is still prized, but more covert. A wonderful monograph, entitled *Doing, Not Doing* says:

> *These [transpersonal] therapies still seem to be based on the traditional cornerstone that the therapist is at least covertly in charge and must somehow direct the flow of the therapeutic outcome. Even so-called new paradigm models couch this essential relationship (therapist as expert) in non-traditional and somewhat "alternative" terminology. For example "I (the therapist) am only a channel. It is not myself doing the healing; it is really God. I am not using my intellect; I am intuitively tuning in on the client's essence, etc."*[97]

Jeanne Achterberg in her book, *Imagery in Healing*, discusses the work of Lawrence LeShan, explaining:

> *The healer doesn't try to do anything to the healee; he/she merely tries to unite, merge, become one with him or her. Deep, intense caring or love focused on the healee is described as the heart of the healing mechanism. . . . it is enough just to "be" there with*

*the expressed purpose of healing in order for healing
to occur.*[98]

Not-doing is not as easy as it sounds. Mastery in this kind of
work is essentially skillful not-doing, Even though therapists are
doing exactly the right thing in nonordinary state work by *not-
doing,* they may still doubt themselves. This attitude can be mir-
rored by a client who is also feeling in strange territory in nonordinary reality and is quick to introject any feeling that all is not
happening as it should.

If we as caregivers are afraid of the spontaneous, transformative energy of nonordinary states, our own fear may stop the client's process by resonating with the client's fear of personal or
transpersonal power. We may communicate verbally, kinestheti-
cally, emotionally, or intuitively to the client that it is dangerous to
proceed. Or perhaps we communicate that it is dangerous to proceed *without us*. In such a case, our carefully controlled boundaries are more for our own benefit than our clients.

■ *A client wants to go on a vision quest, but the
therapist (who would be scared to sleep alone
in the mountains) tells the client she is not
ready for such a powerful experience.*

Even if therapists do not believe they *should* know where a
client's process is going, they might fear the unexpected. They
may resist being surprised, and may try to control the client's
process rather than risk that the unknown might occur in their
offices.

Transference related to power

The client may attribute all the activity in her process to the
magic of the therapist. The therapist can become the archetype of
Magician, the creator of strange worlds, the one who channels energies, and the bringer of the marvelous. *The Bible* talks about this
kind of temptation in describing Christ's offer from the Devil.[99]
The Devil proposed to give Christ vast powers. The client offers to

attribute the vast mystery and power of nonordinary reality to her therapist. Christ declined, but prominent spiritual leaders have often stumbled over this great temptation. In addition to clergy, therapists and bodyworkers are quite vulnerable as well. They may be tempted to own power that is not theirs to claim.

A client is having incredible transpersonal experiences. Nothing in her cultural training or previous life experience prepared her for these possibilities in human experience. The experiences began in a hypnosis session with her therapist. For her, the therapist has taken on the role of Pavlov's bell. Because the nurturing spiritual food of nonordinary states is available in the presence of this therapist, the therapist became the conditioning and, in the client's mind, the catalyst for or the cause of these experiences.

Adolf Guggenbühl-Craig, a Jungian psychotherapist, pointed this out as early as 1971 when he wrote his wonderful book *Power in the Helping Professions*. He warns:

> *The patient's sorcerer-and-apprentice fantasies have a very powerful effect on the therapist, in whose unconscious the figure of the magician or savior begins to be constellated. The therapist starts to think that he is in fact someone with supernatural powers, capable of working wonders with his magic.*[100]

Whenever caregivers claim a power that is not theirs in the therapeutic relationship, they disempower. In reality, they are not healers. Healing occurs in their presence—because they stay out of the way, or because they encourage the client to allow what wants to happen. The experience and the healing, however, are not of their *doing*.

The power center also has its own version of co-dependency. The caregiver may *want* to be the *Healer* and the *Magician*. If he accepts this transference he may have placed himself on the Karpman Drama Triangle[101] as the *Rescuer*. In the Drama Triangle the three roles of *Rescuer*, *Persecutor*, and *Victim* are interchangeable. If someone is playing any one of the three, he may suddenly find himself playing one of the other roles, because the roles are inextricably linked. In the case where the Rescuer is the Magician and bringer of marvelous rescuing worlds, the client is the Victim because she has disempowered herself. The client discounts her own inner wisdom, internal Magician, or Higher Power when she projects the role outside herself onto her caregiver.

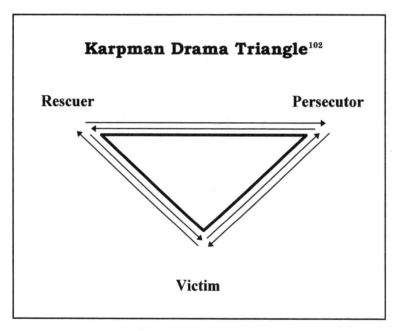

The client is also a Victim because she has been betrayed by her caregiver. The caregiver accepted the projection and did not return it at once. In effect he did not say, *this is not mine, the Magician is a part of you*. Because the caregiver has kept what is not his and has thereby disempowered the client, he has switched from being the Rescuer to being the Persecutor. The client may realize at some point that the caregiver has not acted in the client's best interests but out of the caregiver's own need to be seen as a healer. When she realizes this, the client may well take on the role of Persecutor, leaving the caregiver in the role of Victim.

The caregiver can also take on the Victim role if the client's process becomes difficult. If the caregiver has accepted the role of Magician, then the client is justified in blaming the caregiver if the caregiver does not continue to produce a pleasant, therapeutic experience for the client. The client can also hold the caregiver responsible if the client enters a period of rapid, psychospiritual growth and becomes temporarily dysfunctional in ordinary reality. The client may feel the caregiver could do something to ameliorate the situation and willfully chooses not to do so. The client might switch suddenly to believing that the caregiver is not a magician after all, but is actually ineffectual, even as a caregiver.

The client who has been playing the Victim role also often switches to Persecutor when his resentment against a caregiver builds to a certain point. The client can become angry about being patronized, infantilized or otherwise kept in a one-down position. If this happens, then the roles may change so that the caregiver is the Victim.

Fortunately, if we caregivers are aware of the Drama Triangle, then knowing the consequences of becoming a Persecutor or Victim may keep us from jumping too quickly into the attractive role of Rescuer.

Using the energy of power appropriately

A caregiver working with energy in the power center can validate his own deep longings to assist other people and make a contribution to their lives. He can affirm both his calling to do such work and his deep, caring motivations.

The therapist can use the power of her position in the therapeutic relationship to provide permission when a client feels hesitant to go beyond what he knows. She can encourage a client to dare to enter a nonordinary state again after an experience that has changed his worldview. The therapist can tell the client that she will be with him as he ventures into unknown territory. The therapist can share her fantasy of the client's potential for empowerment and her fantasy of the client's ability to use power creatively and wisely in his life.

A therapist can offer protection when a client feels fear. Alternately, she can reassure the client that if the client does not feel ready, it may not be time to go further. The therapist can use her therapeutic skills and power to differentiate between hesitation and fear so that she provides permission or protection appropriately.

The therapist can examine and challenge herself about her own hesitancies and fears. She can take personal and spiritual risks in her own life to ensure that she continues to communicate courage and trust in the process by her example. A caregiver in the following situation decides she needs to take the next step in her process by going on a spiritual retreat:

■ *I know that I have been thinking a lot about death and am fantasizing having some major illness. I have decided, instead of resisting this or externalizing the process (maybe actually contributing to the creation of illness), I will go further into my fear. I have decided to do two things: start getting regular therapy and attend a ten day meditation retreat.*

The caregiver can do all she can to empower the client, to show the client the strengths, abilities, and gifts which lie within him. She can reflect to the client the client's positive impact upon the caregiver and others. Sometimes the therapist can take the opportunity to reframe nonordinary "problems" as skills or gifts. The client often feels a sense of being special because of his nonordinary experiences. This can effectively increase his self-esteem, as long as he does not take it to the extreme of feeling omnipotent or moving toward megalomania. The caregiver can take care to tell the truth about "being special" and at the same time encourage the client to function well in ordinary consciousness. For example:

■   *You may have been given a special opportunity to develop and heal so that you can better contribute to
others.*

■   *You are developing a wonderful ability to tune in and
receive all kinds of information. All human beings
have the potential to develop psychic abilities, but
not all do, just as some people become musicians and
others do not.*

■   *You have a natural ease in learning how to receive
and interpret information and also the essential
willingness to practice your own spiritual discipline.*

Caregivers can *turn it over* to a Higher Power

Some caregivers have their own Higher Power, a certain
spiritual figure or other source of inspiration to whom they can
surrender their own attachments to specific results. Such an inspi-
rational figure "takes on" the burden of the personal fears and desires so that the seeker can transcend them. The Third Step of the
Twelve Steps involves the decision to turn over one's will (control
or power) to God as one understands God. Other spiritual systems
may use the phrase *give it to the Guru* or *turn it over to Jesus.*

When the client persists in transferring her spiritual power to
the caregiver, the caregiver has no real control over that client
transference. The caregiver can in his own heart, however, pass on
the devotion or whatever has been transferred to him. He can offer
this up to his own source of inspiration so that neither the caregiver nor client remains stuck on the Karpman Drama Triangle. If
the caregiver can quietly and truly disown any spiritual power
transference, the transitional transference period may even be
therapeutic in the same way that any well-managed, parent transference might be.

A caregiver can provide the client with an expanded sense of
what is possible and what is normal in the human experience
of nonordinary states. The caregiver's own experience, mastery of

technique, and ability to act with courage enable him to provide potent permission and protection to his clients.

Therapeutically, the caregiver uses her authority to validate client insights, role-modeling a way for the client to validate and empower herself. She uses her therapeutic techniques to assist the client in amplifying messages. The caregiver does not interpret the client's metaphors but rather helps the client to hear, feel, and interpret her own messages herself. For example:

■ *When you come back to ordinary reality you are denying that your experience with a protective bear was real and you doubt that you even had that experience. It is difficult to value and accept nonordinary reality as real because of our upbringing in modern culture. You might try enacting your power animal to honor the real, nonordinary experience you have had with it.*

■ *You said you saw in your journey a vision of an egg which was beginning to crack. Could you draw another picture to show what is happening to the egg now?*

■ *You said you have a very tight spot in the middle of your body. Would you listen to hear what sound or words that spot might have to express? Could you express that sound for that spot?*

In the above examples, the therapist uses her knowledge of the maps of consciousness, shamanic practice, or mythology to support what is already happening in the client's process. Being careful not to limit or inhibit a process, the therapist provides enough information to validate, give permission for, and normalize what is happening. Using this power of information can help the client chart his way in the unknown territory of nonordinary states. A therapist charting the course of right relationship to power avoids the roles of Rescuer or Magician. Knowing that the therapist is not the *doer*, he returns any projected power to the client, validating the client's inner wisdom, inner healer, Higher Power as the source of the nonordinary, healing experiences which are occurring. In the case where it is not possible to return the transference, the therapist, for his own ethical health, both mental and emotional, can pass it on to some higher spiritual source until the client is ready to reclaim whatever is the client's own. That is, the therapist realizes that he is not the Magician. If there is a Magician to name, he prefers to place that title on some Higher Power than to allow it to stay with him and seduce his own ego. In doing this, he is not disowning his countertransference. Rather, he acknowledges it and actively does something to prevent his believing that the client's view of him as a Magician is accurate.

If the caregiver encounters some process which he fears or which he finds himself trying to control or halt, he might seek consultation. In the spirit of facing his own fear so that he can have integrity in helping the client face fear, he might identify the personal risk he is not taking in his own life and step forward to meet it.

Self-reflection on power

- Do I trust the process (especially in this case)?

- Am I hesitant or fearful about taking a personal or spiritual risk in my own life right now?

- Do I feel that it is dangerous for this client to follow her process wherever it leads?

- Am I empowering the client by amplifying her experiences, metaphors, and insights? Or am I limiting or inhibiting her power by interpreting for her?

- Do I feel as if I should, as the client's caregiver, second-guess or control her experiences?

- Do I feel able to differentiate when the client needs permission from when she needs protection regarding her nonordinary state experiences?

- Do I want my client to think I am responsible for her experiences?

- Do I feel I *am* responsible for her experiences?

- Do I feel attracted to being the Rescuer, the Healer, or the Magician?

- Do I feel as if I have suddenly taken on the role of Persecutor or Victim in relationship to my client?

- Have I passed on any spiritual power transference (which I cannot return to my client right now) to my own higher spiritual source?

Cross-referencing power issues with issues in the other centers

It is possible to exploit the power imbalance that is inherent in a relationship between caregiver and client through any of the issues of the centers. Exploitation is a manipulation of power for the benefit of one party at the expense of the other. We can use power to comfort our feelings of insufficiency or gain sexual favors.

Power can be the driving motivation for spiritual attainment, as when a person seeks to prove to herself she can control her body through yogic austerities, when she seeks to prove to others she "heal" or "fix" others through her special skills, or when she tries to prove she is more compassionate, or more psychic than others. Power issues seem often to go hand in hand with issues of sex and insight. (See *Chapters 6* and *10.*) One might also refer to the section on the use of defense mechanisms by caregivers in *Chapter 13.*

Love—The fourth center

After the third center is the beginning of an adventure beyond the known and into connection with what is beyond the separate self. The personal centers are money, sex, and power. They concern our known identities as separate selves.

The four transpersonal centers (identity and connection outside the separate self) begin with love as it is experienced in the fourth center. Christina Grof wrote, "the opening of the heart, the birth of compassion and love from within, is often the beginning of the true spiritual life.[103]

Countertransference—Spiritual longings and fears related to love

The fourth center (love) is where people move beyond their personal, separate identities. Love opens the heart. In this center the heart easily enfolds another's joys and sorrows within itself. The heart feels what is outside itself as if all were inside.

We long to connect with something or someone beyond ourselves—beyond what Alan Watts called our *skin-encapsulated egos*. While constricted by the troubled, narrow world of personal concerns, we long for this kind of spiritual connection. We long for transcendence beyond the constriction of money, sex, and power issues.

A client often first begins to express the energy of the fourth center after much struggle through issues of the first three centers. Sometimes, after a particular crisis or a powerful release of energy, she suddenly surrenders. Surrender seems to come as an experience of grace, rather than something she feels she has earned or struggled to achieve. Being in the presence of a client experiencing the expansiveness of love energy is similar to attending a home birth. There is an atmosphere created akin to when a baby is born to conscious parents who honor the arrival of a soul into their care.

There is a sacredness, a holiness about the client who, in experiencing fourth center love, feels reborn and honors herself—her *being*. When a client is feeling the movement of energy in the fourth center, she is not in the mode of *doing*, but of *being*. She feels a sense of connection to herself, to her caregiver, to nature, and to everything she contemplates.

A therapist or pastor who observes this serenity and ecstasy may yearn to follow his client into the fourth center. The therapist may long to be fully compassionate, rather than judgmental or indiscriminately accepting, rather than critical. He may wish to feel that quality of open-heartedness. If the caregiver is not able to follow his client into a place of compassion, he remains in a state of longing. He might at this point encounter certain spiritual fears as well as spiritual longings.

The minister or therapist may fear that he cannot be as spiritually connected as his client is. He may despair of feeling the grace of true surrender. He may feel jealous of his client's spiritual birth and natural compassion. He may be jealous of his client's new sense of passionate, spiritual connection. The fear may connect him back to the first center issue of insufficiency.

■ *I am not a good pastor if I am not always spiritually connected—if I am not always naturally compassionate!*

A caregiver may respond inappropriately to a client who is acting naturally and lovingly. The client may seek acknowledgment from the caregiver of the intimacy the client feels between them. Because of her own fear of intimacy, the caregiver may avoid eye contact or distract the client from a moment of heart connection by verbalizing a cognitive thought.

Crossing the bridge between the third and fourth centers means relinquishing the fear of deep connection and intimacy. If one is no longer identified with separateness, one is not afraid of the connection between separate selves. Conversely if the caregiver continues to identify herself as a separate being in the moment—one who is afraid of intimacy—her own constriction may close in upon the expansive, unfolded, and vulnerable heart of the client experiencing love.

If a client's energy moves into the love center while in a nonordinary state of consciousness, the spiritual countertransference can be more confusing. The caregiver may also enter the expansive and spiritually loving state because of the magnetic power of the client's energy. Through the rapport of their relationship, the caregiver may find herself fulfilling her spiritual longings to feel limitless compassion or freedom from the constriction of personal identities.

What happens after the session depends on whether the caregiver had one foot in ordinary reality while accompanying her client into these realms. If the caregiver is unfamiliar with those feelings of fourth center love, then she, as well as the client, may attribute them each to the other or to their relationship. She may become attached to fulfilling her spiritual longings for spiritual connection through her client, or through repeatedly accompanying her client on excursions into nonordinary reality.

Countertransference—Personal desires and fears related to love

The client's outpouring of love and intimacy may fill an empty place inside the caregiver. The caregiver may have an unfulfilled desire to be cherished. She may feel nurtured by the client's ability to merge, feel, and appreciate her unique qualities as a caregiver and as a person. The degree of ethical vulnerability is relative to the degree of unfulfilled need. The caregiver may confuse the opening of the client's feelings of spiritual love (the Greek word *agape* describes this quality) with personal love in ordinary relationship. She may feel special because of her client's gratitude. If the client is in a nonordinary state of consciousness, the caregiver may confuse the gratitude of the client for his reconnection to love and to himself, with a personal love for the caregiver.

Transference related to love

The client may feel that the therapy session is the only place where he can leave behind the constriction of personal desires, fears, and concerns about money, sex, and power. He may feel that the therapy session is the only place he can feel expansive and ecstatic. He may likewise decide that his caregiver is the only person with whom he can experience love.

A psychiatrist offered this case as an example of both countertransference and transference in the area of love taken from an in-patient psychiatric setting. The following case is also a good illustration of the lure of the Rescuer role and how, if accepted, it can skew therapy.

■ *A 38-year-old never married Caucasian male was sent to the hospital for psychiatric evaluation from the jail where he was being held on child molestation charges. He was guilty and this was a repeat offense.*

He was from a highly dysfunctional but highly achieving family. His father had been an unavailable rigid lawyer holding state office. His mother was an infantilizing neurotic. His younger brother was a practicing psychoanalyst.

During the course of a process group on the ward, the patient for the first time in his life expressed his primal rage and in the process broke a piece of furniture. He was terrified and regressed to a child-like state and began to sob. I held him in my arms in the center of the group and he went from sobbing to an ecstatic state, radiating joy. (My construction: the child was not punished for breaking the furniture.)

Later I took a lot of flack for the broken table and the patient heard of it. He decided that I was his savior, and I, not in those grandiose terms, thought I could help him. I invested a lot of time and eventually persuaded the court to move him from the state hospital for the criminally insane to a local institution where I could treat him.

We entered into treatment and after one week, he escaped! So much for my savior role and the feelings of love that he had during that process group!

It is obvious to me now that I was not aware of my own longings for love and connection, nor of my fear of losing the patient's love and esteem. Thus, I grossly overvalued my skills as a therapist and underrated his pathology. I heard years later that he had again been arrested and imprisoned for repeat child molestation.

Because we do not have more words in our modern languages to distinguish between types and qualities of love, fourth center love, even if experienced purely in the nonordinary state of consciousness, may be remembered differently upon the return to ordinary consciousness. In returning from nonordinary reality to ordinary reality, the client may bring back the concept of love (*agape*) and re-package it as personal love, making his caregiver the object of that love.

Again, the management of such transference depends on the amount of experience the caregiver has had with nonordinary states. Spiritual love, just as any human experience, can be skillfully practiced by a client in a therapy session, using the therapist as a tool and a stand-in so the client can learn to feel and express this kind of love safely in his other present and future relationships.

Using the energy of love appropriately

The client can practice experiencing the state of love in nonordinary states of consciousness unencumbered by ordinary reality with its worries and attachments. She can also practice fully feeling with the fears and longings that emerge as the nonordinary state fades and she returns to her ordinary state of consciousness. The fears of and desires for cherishing, commitment, intimacy, open-heartedness, and appropriate boundaries are all grist for the mill in the therapeutic relationship.

The caregiver can help in setting appropriate boundaries. Angeles Arrien lists six kinds of universal love one of which is *professional love between teacher and student, therapist and client, and so on.*[104] This is different love from the love of a parent for a child or a mate for a lover. For example, a client may want and expect friendship outside the therapeutic relationship after an intimate, heart-merging session. If a caregiver is not clear about his own boundaries, he might opt to close his heart to create the boundary, defending himself in that way in order to keep the client at a distance between sessions. Instead, he could give his client a clear message about how and when he is willing to participate in an intimate relationship with his client:

■ *If you have me for a friend, you would lose a therapist. Let's continue to allow ourselves to be intimate in the context of our therapeutic session. Sometimes it will feel appropriate to touch and other times not. I want to be clear that intimacy does not mean sexuality in this case. I would like to talk with you about what works for us to create intimacy, what feels awkward, what moves us away from intimacy, and how you want to apply these experiences to other relationships in your life.*

Although the caregiver is not responsible for the client's feelings, the caregiver is responsible for her own response to those feelings. Any ambiguity about her willingness to participate physically in a sexual or romantic relationship will threaten the safety of the therapeutic relationship.

In the therapeutic relationship, the boundaries must be sufficiently well-defined, so that both hearts feel enough permission and protection to remain open.

Self-reflection on love

■ Do I feel spiritually lonely?

■ Do I feel as if I have experienced love (*agape*) because of this client?

■ Do I feel as if my client is experiencing love because of me?

■ Have I acknowledged my longing for spiritual connection?

■ Have I acknowledged my deep wish to be compassionate?

■ Am I afraid of intimacy in general? With this client?

- Do I strongly desire intimacy in general? With this particular client?

- How do I withdraw from intimacy?

- Am I jealous of my client's ability to surrender? To feel ecstasy? To feel gratitude? To *be,* without *doing*? To be compassionate?

- Do I feel insufficient as a caregiver because I am not sufficiently connected spiritually or not compassionate enough?

- Is my desire to be cherished unfulfilled at this time?

- Have I been clear with my client about the boundaries to our intimacy?

- How have I established sufficient permission and protection for each of us to be intimate within the therapy session?

- If I am entering a nonordinary state along with my client in these sessions, can I distinguish between the time I am in a nonordinary state of consciousness and when I am in an ordinary state of consciousness? How do I know the difference?

- Am I able to differentiate between transpersonal (*agape*) love and personal love?

Cross-referencing love issues with issues in the other centers

Love, in the fourth center sense, is a nonordinary state of consciousness. Therefore, one might refer to the special needs of a client in a nonordinary state. (See *Chapter 3.*) Also the section in *Chapter 12* which discusses our unacknowledged longings for love and spiritual connection might offer some insights that would be applicable to a particular situation.

Love is often confused with sex (see *Chapter 6*). If there is a savior or Rescuer element to the particular client situation you have in mind, the chapter on power, particularly the section on the Karpman Drama Triangle may be of assistance (see *Chapter 7*). It might be helpful to refer to the sections on authentic caring and willingness to ask for help in *Chapter 13* as well.

9

*T*ruth

What our heart longs for is truth,
but what we can express are merely truths. . . .
Instead of grasping for truths,
we can allow the truth to grasp us. [105]

—Br. David Steindl-Rast

*T*ruth—The fifth center

Clients in nonordinary states of consciousness speak and act honestly. They usually have little inclination or ability to fabricate their thoughts, responses, or actions. They are, temporarily at least, not much interested in lying to fulfill personal desires or protect themselves against personal fears. They are often beyond the ordinary motives which can require manipulation of the truth and of others. What is happening in the nonordinary state is important to them. They act and relate to others with urgent authenticity.

Countertransference—Spiritual longings and fears related to truth

As caregivers, our longing for transcendence manifests in this center as the longing to manifest truth. We long to be above the fears and desires which make us tell little white lies or avoid telling the whole truth. We long to have the pure truth manifest through us. We want our facial expressions to be without artifice, our words not slanted, and our actions to occur without ulterior purpose.

The client in a nonordinary state of consciousness sometimes achieves quickly what meditators strive for—consciousness with no filters to tint or taint pure experience. When a client manifests truth, her energy is free. Even when the truth is emotionally upsetting to her, she may seem, in essence, remarkably peaceful. It is as if her true being were in the eye of the storm around which her body and emotions are temporarily expressing the tempest. The caregiver may long to achieve this same peace.

Countertransference—Personal desires and fears related to truth

The client's actions may seem quite free of conventions. For the moment, obligatory compliments, smiles, giggles, and pleasantries are no longer part of her repertoire. The caregiver, through his own desire to speak and act with more integrity, may be quite drawn to the frank comments and the lack of guile on the part of the client.

The truth is sometimes scary, however. It was probably so for the emperor in the fairy tale when the little boy pointed out to him that he really had no clothes on. Likewise, the client in a nonordinary state of consciousness can unmask the caregiver. The client may see clearly, for example, the caregiver's illusions, personal issues, and motivations. Specifically, the client may verbalize her perception of the caregiver's sexual attraction to the client, jealousy of the client, need to control the client's process, or feelings of insufficiency in the therapy session.

On hearing such perceptions, the caregiver's desire for integrity and freedom from convention may move him to act outside his therapeutic boundaries. Such actions, in some circumstances, could include reversing roles and talking overly much about his own process to the client. He might also indulge himself with regard to a discussion about sexual attraction or even engage in sexual behavior with the client.

On the other hand, the caregiver's reaction to a client speaking such truth about the caregiver might be to conceal whatever the client has identified or seen. Visibility, to the caregiver, can be vulnerability. The caregiver may fear being seen by another, especially by a client. The caregiver may feel that if she admits to the client that the client has spoken accurately, she will lose the client's respect. She may feel she will lose "control" of the therapy. She may spiral into her own family history of shame and guilt if she imagines she has done something "wrong." Because of shame and guilt, she may not even admit to herself that what the client is saying about her is true.

Transference related to truth

Clients often have deep fears from early childhood about telling the truth. They can project their fears onto the caregiver. The client may be afraid of not being believed, being punished, or being criticized. The client can imagine that the caregiver is going to disbelieve, punish, or criticize. This fear may come from experiences in ordinary states of consciousness. Perhaps the child observed something about a family guest and was scolded for doing so. Most of us have this kind of social conditioning regarding our truth-telling.

Alternately, the origin of such fear might stem from a very young age when the client told the truth about his earliest nonordinary state experiences. Perhaps as a child, he had an imaginary playmate, had precognitive knowledge, experienced ESP, or saw auras. If the child related those experiences to adults, it is quite possible that he was ignored, told he was a liar, sent to his room, or even beaten. He was probably told never again to say those kinds of things. Some sensitive children pick up the anxiety of the parent and learn to shut off their own experience to avoid provoking the parent. If the client has had this kind of history, then truth-telling in a nonordinary state may bring him in touch with some powerful, negative parental injunctions. The client can easily project the caregiver into those negative parental roles.

Conversely, the client might transfer onto the caregiver the role of the Good Parent—the one who would have listened to and appreciated her accounts of her nonordinary experiences. The caregiver might investigate in this case what happened to the Bad Parent, which has probably been introjected and may yet reappear in therapy. Again, this is a case where the caregiver might be wary of stepping onto the Karpman Drama Triangle as a Rescuer, only to unwittingly become the Persecutor at a later time. (See *Chapter 7*.)

Some clients have had religious judgments superimposed on their direct spiritual experiences. Adults have told them that certain experiences are scary and wrong. Words such as *witchcraft, devil, evil spirits,* and *ghosts* are sometimes used by adults who are frightened of the nonordinary. These words might be meant to keep children from remembering or reporting their nonordinary experiences.

The client can also project her inner critic onto the caregiver. She may fear saying or doing something wrong. She may have a deep distrust in her own truth. She may be afraid the caregiver will laugh at her reports or simply not believe her. She may think something is wrong with her because she has not heard of anyone else experiencing something similar. The caregiver is a likely screen on which to project those fears.

The client can project responsibility onto the caregiver who induced the nonordinary state in which the client told certain truths. This might be particularly relevant when the nonordinary state puts the client in touch with childhood sexual abuse issues. In many of these cases, children were told that if they told certain truths they would be punished. When they do tell as adults, they may be very frightened of punishment, just as they were as children. Some false memory charges against caregivers may be clients' attempts to avoid responsibility and retribution for telling their truth.

The client telling the truth may be bringing forth metaphoric truth rather than literal truth. Some "false memory" tales of abuse are not historical but are poetic ways to tell a truth, because the real truth cannot be communicated adequately or received fairly in its literal terms. (See *Chapter 3.*)

Using the energy of truth appropriately

The caregiver can encourage the client's truth-telling. Whether the client is uncovering new information about herself, about her experience, or about the caregiver, the caregiver can acknowledge and appreciate the client's authenticity. If the client reveals information about the caregiver that the caregiver would rather the client not have known, the caregiver can take a courageous breath and simply validate what is so. She can help distinguish between what is true for her and what is true for the client, if there is a difference. The caregiver can acknowledge briefly any factual information and any general weaknesses that the client has discovered without dwelling on them. She might also inquire how the client feels about that information, pointing out that the object of the session is to focus on the client's thoughts and feelings.

■   *You are right. I am afraid of taking physical risks. It is something I am working on in my own life. Is that information useful to you in working with me? How does it feel to know your therapist is afraid of physical risks?*

It may be a bigger challenge when the client has brought out some truth about the relationship dynamic between her and her caregiver. It is wonderful if the caregiver is in a position to simply acknowledge the truth and to stay present with the client, encouraging her to continue with her inner explorations.

■ *You are right. I am attracted to you. You are an attractive woman. I will never, however, have a romantic or sexual relationship with you. I take my responsibilities as a therapist very seriously in that regard.*

■ *I am jealous of you sometimes. I wish I had contact with spirit guides as you do. Most of the time I am in sessions with you, however, I am not thinking about that. Mostly, I am feeling happy that you are opening up so much! Right now, I am glad you brought this up so I could acknowledge it.*

■ *You have said you thought I had an agenda for you. Yes, I did want you to get into your anger more and was encouraging you too much in that direction. I can see now that sadness was the emotion which you needed to express. Sometimes I forget that the process has a mind of its own and I am just here to assist it, not to control it.*

If it feels like the therapeutic dialogue is taking a detour because of "truth-telling," it is also an appropriate response sometimes to clarify that the therapy is not focused on the therapist's issues. It can be quite true and therapeutically relevant to say:

■ *We're not here to deal with my issues. You are paying me for this time so that we can both focus on you.*

If the client is in a nonordinary state at the time of the revelation and is insistent upon getting a response to her statements, the therapist has several choices. Much depends on the content and how vulnerable the therapist feels to the particular issue that the client has broached. If the therapist is feeling vulnerable and fears that vulnerability might impair her professional judgment, she can set her boundaries, while promising to return to the issue which the client has brought up. Here are a few suggestions for therapist response in this circumstance:

■ *I want to talk further with you about this when we are both in an ordinary state of consciousness.*

■ *I cannot give this matter the attention it deserves and still stay present with you for the rest of this session. We will talk about this later for sure.*

■ *I am glad you brought this to my attention. There seems to be some truth in it. Let's talk about it some more in another session.*

Profound experiences quite often bring the mythical, perinatal, and archetypal realms into therapy. In a case where the client may tell her myth as literal truth, both the client and the therapist may be bewildered and not know what to believe. It may be helpful to treat such material as inner process while validating the material itself (not necessarily the facts) as real and, in the most profound sense, true. Myth and metaphor can often reveal more subtleties about a client's experience than mere facts. (See *Chapter 3*.)

Truth-telling requires commensurate responsibility. Truth and responsibility go hand in hand. Responsibility is awakened through connection, caring, and love in the fourth center. The spiritual energy in the fourth center is often silent and wordless, but the spiritual energy of love is often expressed outwardly as truthful words and responsible action when it reaches the fifth center.

Self-reflection on truth

■ Do I long to channel wisdom and higher truth?

■ Do I long to speak and act with more integrity?

■ Do I want to be free of conventions and social restrictions?

■ Does my client's truth-telling make me nervous?

■ Have I responded truthfully to my client's insights about me or my motivations?

- In response to my client's questions about me, have I discussed my own process more than was necessary for my client's therapeutic needs?

- Have I crossed any other therapeutic boundaries with this client?

- Am I afraid of being seen by my client?

- Have I validated my client's nonordinary experiences?

- Can I perceive both the possibility of truth in myth and the possibility of fallacy in "fact"?

Cross-referencing truth issues with issues in the other centers

Truth issues may be closely connected to money, sex, and power issues. (See *Chapters 5, 6, and 7.*) Willingness to tell the truth to ourselves, our peers, and our clients is discussed at length in *Chapter 13*.

10

nsight

*I can only stand in deepest awe and admiration
before the depths and heights of the soul
whose world beyond space hides an immeasurable
richness of images . . . . These images are not pale shadows,
but powerful and effective conditions of the soul
which we can only misunderstand
but can never rob of their power by denying them.*

—C. G. Jung

Insight—The sixth center

The sixth center is the traditional seat of the third eye or spiritual insight. The client whose energy is working in this center may spontaneously exhibit what have come to be known as psychic powers. In the yogic tradition these are known as *siddhis* and there are Sanskrit names for each. Some of them include hearing inner sounds and vision and having yogic control of the body.[106] We might see some of these experiences in clients, such as extrasensory perception, voices inside the head, and mystical experiences, including seeing visions of saints and various aspects of God, and gaining deep understanding of spiritual concepts which cannot be transferred to others by verbal means.

A client experiencing psychic phenomena may wonder whether or not these symptoms are signs of serious mental illness or signs of developmental stages along the spiritual path. (See discussion of psychosis versus nonordinary states in *Chapter 2*.) Many religious and psychological professionals might agree that they are signs of psychosis and that anyone who does not treat these phenomena as such is unethical. Yet there is a mystical tradition in each of the world's great religions and in the shamanic traditions which affirms that spiritual development accompanied by these kinds of phenomena *is* different and distinguishable from mental illness.

Countertransference—Spiritual longings and fears related to insight

A therapist whose client is having these kinds of experiences may long to have such psychic powers or mystical experiences himself. He may think of them as some kind of benchmark for spiritual progress and measure himself unfavorably because he has not had them. If he has had some of these experiences in the past, he may long to have them again in the present.

At the same time, the therapist may be afraid of misusing those kinds of spiritual powers if he did have them. If he could read minds, he might feel he would take advantage of people. He might have a fear of seeing too clearly; a fear of knowing the future. He may fear precognition because he is attached to certain outcomes. He may be afraid of consciously experiencing out of body journeys or encountering spirits or archetypal figures in the inner realms.

These spiritual longings and fears can trigger the issues of the other centers (particularly money (change), sex, and power). The therapist may want to control the client's process, join with it (as Magician or Lover), or resist the process because it represents change and loss.

In the case of the sixth center, a therapist may fear losing his ignorance of certain things due to a direct personal encounter with a client having mystical experiences. Ignorance might seem like a good thing to lose, but ignorance can protect us from fear, change, and responsibility. Loss of ignorance might mean that in some way irresponsibility is no longer an option.

Countertransference—Personal desires and fears related to insight

The therapist has a great personal desire to understand the client's therapeutic process. This is almost a requirement for becoming a therapist! In working with clients in nonordinary states of consciousness, the therapist's desire to know the bigger picture is confounded by the great mystery. No one can ever know why things happen a certain way or how they fit into a picture too big for human comprehension. Sometimes in states of nonordinary consciousness, there is a vantage point from which to glimpse larger panoramas. But, especially in ordinary states of consciousness, it is wiser to be humble about our capacity to know what is happening in another's process.

The inexplicable twists and turns of a client's psychospiritual journey confound most attempts to interpret or predict. The therapist's issues in this center may connect to the first center (security) and to the third (power). *Knowing* is a more subtle way of trying to exert control and to resist the unknown which is change.

The personal fears involved with the therapist's countertransference in this center might include fear of losing denial as a defense mechanism. The client's existential understanding may break through the therapist's denial of the transitory nature of life and of her own mortality. She may resist knowing what the client has brought back from his nonordinary journey and so may unconsciously discount the client's insights.

The therapist's fear of misusing spiritual powers if she should acquire them herself may be transferred inappropriately to the client. When a client receives certain spiritual abilities, he is usually given an understanding of how these gifts are to be used or not used. The therapist, however, may not have the benefit of that understanding and fear the client's use of such "powers."

Aleister Crowley, occult theorist, felt there was a universal principle: *Do what thou wilt is the whole of the law.* From certain viewpoints (for example in the third center, power), this frightens us. In the third center, we may regard ourselves as separate beings who "win" at the expense of other separate beings.

In nonordinary states (especially when energy is working with insight), we may shed various layers of this kind of ignorance. In these states we may understand that everyone has the power to co-create his life. We realize we can use this power with knowledge. In other words, we experience wisdom which has shed the ignorance from which we would misuse this power. In this place we can more easily feel the consequences of our actions to others in the web of life because we feel one with them. *Do unto others as you would have them do unto you* can become a living axiom. We realize there is no real winning possible unless the *other* wins also.

If the therapist finds herself cautioning the client about the dangers of psychic powers, contact with spirits, or out of body experiences, she might reflect on the source of her concern. If she does not have much experience with these states or experiences, she may not be able to sort out which therapeutic advice is balancing and spiritually sound and which is coming from her own fears or ignorance.

Transference related to insight

Upon acquiring psychic gifts or insights, the client may assume that the therapist already possesses or understands these. This assumption may weigh heavily on the therapist if she wishes to appear enlightened.

The client may, again in this center as in the power center, feel that the therapist makes it possible for him to have these experiences. If it were not for the therapist, he feels he would have none of these insights, mystical experiences, or psychic abilities. He may feel dependent on this particular therapist's hypnotic induction, drumming, or his presence in order to encounter these realms in himself.

Using the energy of insight appropriately

With the deep knowledge that he is not the doer, the caregiver does not expect to know how the process will unfold or where it will take the client. He trusts the process, meaning that he has had his own deep experience of the healing nature of nonordinary states. He knows, from his own experience and the experiences of others with whom he has worked, that even the rapid, tumultuous feelings and events of psychospiritual crisis eventually result in greater healing and greater peace. The caregiver knows from his own training and experience that those who go through the spiritual emergence process return from their intense experiences (even from periods of dysfunction) with greater ability to function. They bring back valuable, new gifts to their community.

A female client brought back a new set of priorities in which she now "puts people before tasks." She was mistakenly diagnosed as bi-polar when she had an experience of rapturous identity with a goddess while visiting a traditional sacred site. After a difficult time of dysfunction and integration, she has come to terms with her experience as a spiritual one that shifted her priorities in life. She now has more compassion for other people and greater rapport with her many students. She describes herself as a highly functioning person who has always accomplished a great deal by keeping a driving focus on her goals. She now says, "I always put down 'tasks' in order to spend time with people who need me."

If the client mistakenly assumes that the caregiver understands her process, has had the same kinds of experiences, and is able to demonstrate the same psychic abilities, the caregiver can tell her the truth. If the caregiver has not had the same kinds of experiences as his client, he can suggest that both he and the client do some reading about these. He can reiterate that he has had enough experience with *not knowing* to place his trust in the natural unfolding of each person's spiritual development.

> ■ *I have not had the particular experience you are having. I have had, however, enough of my own nonordinary experiences to trust that your inner wisdom will give you appropriate guidance as you go along. How has it given you this guidance so far?*

Self-reflection on insight

- ■ Have I acknowledged my longing for mystical experiences?

- ■ Am I fascinated by the demonstration of psychic powers?

- ■ Do I think that spiritual advancement is measured in psychic powers?

- ■ Does my client think I have experienced or know more than I really do?

- ■ Am I comparing myself to my client to see who is more spiritually advanced?

- ■ Have I been cautioning my client about the possible dangers of these experiences?

- ■ Am I afraid of some of the experiences my client is having?

■ Am I encouraging my client to produce more "spiritual" experiences because I am fascinated by them?

■ Do the phenomena which the client is experiencing have symbolic meaning within the therapeutic relationship and the transference?

■ Do I resist feeling the emotional impact of certain existential issues, such as transience and mortality, or pain and suffering?

■ Do I think that I might misuse spiritual or psychic abilities if I had them? How might I do that?

■ Do I want to thoroughly understand and predict my client's process? My own process?

■ Do I feel an inclination to control or slow down what is happening with my client or myself?

■ Have I communicated to my client a basic trust in the spiritual process which is unfolding in her? If not, what am I communicating to her about trusting her process?

Cross-referencing insight with issues in the other centers

Insight may relate back to the personal centers (see *Chapters 5, 6,* and *7*). Fear of change or insufficiency can certainly be an issue when a client has powerful, spiritual experiences. Sex can be involved as a longing for tantric and mystical sex. Power becomes an issue in this center as well if the caregiver has been given or has taken on the role of Magician or facilitator of the psychic or mystical experiences.

Particularly relevant may be the section on countertransference with a client's psychic opening in *Chapter 12*. If a client is having these kinds of experiences, the next chapter on oneness might also be applicable.

11

neness

*One can connect with a state that feels eternal,
understanding that one is at once the body
and also all that exists.*

—Christina and Stanislav Grof

Oneness—The seventh center

The deepest longings we have are to wake up to our identity
with something bigger than ourselves. Many people call that
something *God*. Even if we are not religious, something in us
longs to feel that we are eternal. We long to feel connected to
spirit, however we understand that term. We long to feel the liberation of our material selves merged with spirit, our mortal selves

connected to the immortal. Our yearnings that were awakened as the longing for the unchangeable in the first center have their fulfillment in seventh center experiences. I have titled the seventh center *oneness*, but it could also be called unity consciousness.

Countertransference—Spiritual longings and fears related to oneness

A client who experiences the energy of this center is often either:

1) A long-time spiritual practitioner;

2) In the midst of a spontaneous, powerful spiritual emergence or spiritual emergency;

3) Using a consciousness-expanding substance or other catalyst to do vision-questing; or

4) Dying.

Ministers and hospice workers encounter these experiences when their parishioners or patients are in the final stages of the death process. Meditation teachers may encounter them in students during a retreat. Jack Kornfield reminds us in his book, *A Path With Heart*, "Awakening is not far away; it is nearer than near."[107]

Such experiences have occurred for people on vision quests, in churches, in psychedelic sessions, during childbirth, during sex, and in hospitals. The following is an account by Katy Butler, who experienced what she calls her "small, spiritually healing experience" at the Most Holy Redeemer Church in San Francisco, while contemplating the silver container (monstrance) that held communion wafers on the altar:

For years I had felt so damaged that I thought I should hide myself. But the god I sensed glimmering from the monstrance included everything, even me. How could I hide from the universe when I was part of it? Connection was possible, even though I could only barely sense it. I did not need to hide any more; there was nowhere to hide, and nothing to hide. My shame was a delusion; it came from inside, not outside.[108]

Butler said that her therapist did not reduce her experience to psychological terms, but instead affirmed what had happened and added that such experiences had been excluded from the therapeutic universe for too long. Butler reported that after the experience she,

> *no longer felt like a cripple fashioning a better set of crutches. I knew things could be different, and I also knew I would have to face my memories if I wished to deepen that fleeting vision into something I could live each day. The lid of shame was off.*[109]

Here is another story of such a spontaneous visit to the seventh center. It occurred in a psychiatric ward in what we now know enough to classify as a spiritual emergency rather than a psychosis. The experience has remained with Deane Brown, psychologist and retired Director of the Spiritual Emergence Network, and has continued to inspire her work and her life.

■ *I shot to a place beyond words, beyond symbols, beyond imagery—a place of nothingness, but a nothingness in which all the knowledge of what is and what can be and what will be lay, a nothingness in which I was light waiting to shine, sound pulsating to be born. I passed through the levels of reality between the material world and a pure energy, a state in which every cell in my body became orgasmic. I saw my body encapsulated in words, defined, restricted, limited by words. And in going where I went I burst out of these word bonds into an infinity of wordlessness and timelessness, an infinity of love, of ecstasy, of bliss, of "the peace that passeth all understanding." I was—and am—one with the universe; I am the universe; God and I are one.*[110]

The therapist's deepest longings and deepest doubts may be unlocked by a client who has journeyed beyond her separate, transient self. The therapist may feel a surge of hope. Hope in the prospect of eternal life in the spirit exists side by side with a deep spiritual fear of the transformation (and loss) of a therapist's known and separate identity. This transition from separate self to becoming one with all is as fundamental as the transformation of a fetus into a baby at birth. New life, in human form or in spirit form, requires surrender (death) of the old form. New spiritual consciousness is so similar to physical birth that some spiritual traditions use the birth imagery to describe this *born again* experience. Indeed, Deane Brown goes on to say:

> *I found that I was extremely sensitive to what other*
> *people were thinking and feeling; their thoughts and*
> *emotions were as clear to me as their physical bod-*
> *ies. With wonder, I thought, "This is the kind of vul-*
> *nerability that newborn infants must have. Is that*
> *what people mean by being born again?"*[111]

There are Sanskrit words which differentiate between kinds of advanced states of meditation. In *sabija* or *salvikalpa samadhi* (samadhi with the seed of desire), the meditator is attached to having the subject-object or knower-known distinction. This state corresponds to the sixth center. The meditator is attached to loving God as an *other*. The higher *nirbija* or *nirvakalpa samadhi* is the one in which the mind dissolves and duality disappears.[112] This experience is one in which there is no *other*, only the one of which we each are a part. This kind of samadhi is the experience of oneness (seventh center). This passage describes the awakening process: "In your dreams, in your desires, you are asleep. And the reality is here and now. Once this sleep has been broken—the dream has been broken and you become awakened to the reality that is here and now, in the present—you are reborn. You come to ecstasy, to fulfillment, to all that has always been desired but never achieved."[113]

The response of the caregiver to a client who has experienced oneness may vary. The caregiver's response tends to depend on which center's issues are current for the caregiver. If the caregiver's energies are moving in the transpersonal centers (fourth, fifth, and sixth), her responses probably will not be motivated by personal fears and desires. She may feel openhearted and loving (fourth). Without having the need to understand exactly what is happening, she might validate the authenticity (fifth) of her client's experience.

If the caregiver is currently experiencing the energies of the sixth center in her own spiritual practice, she might feel her own internal conflict. On the one hand, she may want to continue feeling the ecstasy of loving God as *other* in her meditations, but may fear losing the object of her devotion in surrendering to an experience of oneness. On the other hand, she may want to develop spiritually and experience nonduality but may fear venturing out of the known and losing herself as the knower and experiencer.

Countertransference—Personal desires and fears related to oneness

If the caregiver's own energies are currently moving in the personal centers (first, second, and third), rather than the transpersonal centers, she may relate differently to a client who is experiencing cosmic unity. Some themes arising may be desire for merging or dissolving boundaries and fear of losing one's self identity.

The caregiver may enjoy the temporary dissolution of boundaries which often happens between people when one or more of them is experiencing a nonordinary state of consciousness. She may become attached to the dissolution of personal boundaries and lose her ability to return cleanly and fully to ordinary consciousness and to separate selves, roles, and lives.

Here again, there is a danger of mixing levels. Both caregiver and client can try to fulfill their desire for dissolution of barriers between separate selves by merging with each other, rather than dissolving separations internally and spiritually.

If the caregiver is concerned primarily with the first center (money and security) she may be intrigued but mostly fearful of experiencing such change. If she is working with second center issues of sex, she might be attracted physically to the client as a way to acquire the client's state of being. If she is currently being challenged by power issues in the third center, she might feel left out of the experience or feel out of control with the therapy. Conversely, in a megalomaniac way, she might believe she was the cause of the client's experience.

Transference related to oneness

The client who is presently experiencing a cosmic unity does not have transference issues. Transference issues may arise if the client comes back to ordinary consciousness or a less conscious level of awareness. Unless the oneness experience is occurring in a dying client, the client does return to ordinary consciousness and resumes ordinary life. The task then may be to integrate the wordless, profound experience of discovering one's true nature with the ordinary perspective of life as a separate being bound by time and space.

The client as well as the caregiver is in danger of confusing levels. The client can project godhead archetypes on the caregiver. Transference in this way can connect the client back to the second center so that the client confuses her desire to merge with the Divine Lover with her desire for physical union and partnership.[114] The caregiver may become the target of misplaced divine adoration. The caregiver may indeed be divine but no more divine than anyone or anything else.

The client may try to fulfill his desire for union with the caregiver, rather than keeping his focus internal. He, as well as the caregiver, may confuse the archetypal sacred marriage with external union or dependency. The sacred marriage is a psychospiritual metaphor for the internal union of the masculine and feminine parts of the psyche and by extended metaphor for the union of all duality.

This confusion about what is the sacred marriage can happen especially if the client's process has involved reconnecting to his body. In the kundalini type of spiritual emergence, for example, the spiritual energy moving through him as bodily energy wants a way to express itself. Sex can be both physical and spiritual or a metaphor for the spiritual union.

The client who has recently gained a perspective of the divinity of everything may fear losing that perspective. He may try to succeed in focusing divinity in one place (on the caregiver) instead of failing to keep his perspective of the divinity of everything.

Using the energy of oneness appropriately

When the caregiver sees a client who has recently had an experience of oneness, the most valuable therapeutic approach may be to receive and honor that experience. Certainly listening to the client tell his story is important. The client may not have very many people in his life with whom he can share this experience. A caregiver who can intuit how profound this consciousness-changing experience is for the client and who can infuse her listening with love, enthusiasm, and reverence will provide crucial support during this *newborn* time. The caregiver's nonjudgmental and empathetic reception of the client's sacred feelings can be a great gift.

The caregiver can validate the client's experiences, if appropriate, by telling stories of similar sacred experiences of union, perhaps referring her to yogic texts or the biographies of saints.[115] She might also use the metaphor of birth to assist the client in assimilating her experience.

The client's task after a seventh center experience is to live what she has understood. Sanskrit has a term for a third type of samadhi (*sahaj samadhi* or open-eyed samadhi). In this state there is said to be no difference between the inner bliss of nonordinary states and the outer bliss of ordinary consciousness. There is nothing but one constant state of samadhi. Although very few people are known to awaken to this state, those who have had a oneness experience can bring it into daily life in a variety of ways. The person often feels a responsibility to carry this kind of profound experience into the world. People who have had these experiences understand that statement, although they may appreciate being reminded of it.

A caregiver might suggest to the client that he find a tradition that has time-tested practices for helping people change their lives to correspond with their new spiritual knowledge. She may recommend that the client undertake that discipline in order to make use in ordinary reality of what he found in nonordinary consciousness.

If the client is transferring the archetype of Divine Lover onto the caregiver, the caregiver can sometimes reframe the client's longings for the caregiver as the client reaching for the relationship he most wants, be it human, divine, or the inner "marriage" of his most polarized selves.

The caregiver can identify for herself how she is relating to this client's oneness experience. The caregiver can locate her own issues on the chart (Caregiver Vulnerabilities to Ethical Misconduct), which is shown inside the back cover of this book, and find information that would be helpful in the chapters about those centers. Once she has identified and worked with her attachments in the personal centers, she may work more easily with energy in the transpersonal centers and relate to her client's transpersonal orientation with enhanced empathy. The caregiver can also try to determine, perhaps with the help of consultation, if she is confusing transpersonal with personal levels of experience or nonordinary states of consciousness with ordinary states of consciousness.

If the client has a seventh center experience while in the presence of the caregiver, the caregiver can provide the same quality of welcoming reception to the client as to a newborn at a conscious birthing. Silence is usually an important part of honoring the experience while it happens.

Self-reflection on oneness

- Did I listen to the story of my client's oneness experience with empathy and encouragement?

- Did the client feel that her experience was honored and held sacred by me?

- Do I feel comfortable being with a client who is currently having an experience of oneness? If not, why? What might I be resisting?

- What issues of which centers were active for me as I heard my client's story?

- Do I have a belief system that can include experiences of cosmic unity or oneness with God?

- In my own meditation or religious practice, am I attached to worshipping God as an *other*?

- Do I have a tendency to confuse the sacred marriage of internal union with the union of external relationship?

- Does my client see me, to any degree, as the Divine Lover?

- Do I feel comfortable moving back and forth between nonordinary and ordinary reality? If so, which is more difficult to leave?

- Am I attracted or repelled by merging experiences and the dissolution of boundaries between people?

Cross-referencing oneness with issues in the other centers

Oneness or cosmic consciousness is the supreme nonordinary state of consciousness. In *Chapter 2* one can review what such a state is and the role of awareness in nonordinary states. The client who experiences oneness may have a particular need for help in making the transition back to ordinary consciousness. The section integrating profound experiences in *Chapter 3* may be of some assistance.

12

Vulnerabilities to Unethical Behavior

Concerning our human vulnerabilities, Christina Grof wrote, "I like the image conveyed by the original meaning of the word pitfall. It is a lightly camouflaged hole in the ground that hunters use to ensnare animals or that the enemy employs to capture members of the opposition. On the spiritual journey, we slip into many pitfalls, and the enemy is usually ourselves."[116]

This chapter names conditions which make a therapist or caregiver more vulnerable to stepping off the track of right relationship into the pitfalls of unethical behavior. These include both conscious and unconscious disregard for the client, therapist or caregiver burnout, ignorance on the part of the caregiver about the ethical pitfalls, and underestimation of the force of a client's nonordinary states, her experiences in them, and the power of her transference to affect the caregiver. These vulnerabilities also include the unexamined personal fears, desires, and longings that comprise countertransference.

Vulnerabilities to Unethical Behavior

■ Disregard for the client

■ Caregiver burnout

■ Ignorance of the pitfalls

■ Underestimation of the power of nonordinary states of consciousness (and transference) to affect us

■ Our own unexamined personal issues (countertransference)

■ Our unacknowledged longings (countertransference) for love and spiritual connection

Disregard for the client

The most obvious vulnerability is disregard for the client. There are two types of such disregard: willful, calculated disregard and unconscious disregard.

I cannot imagine that anyone interested in expanding ethical consciousness (anyone reading this book, for example) would fall into behavior of the first type. A caregiver who willfully and purposefully disregards the best interests of his client in order to meet his own desires or needs is not interested in avoiding pitfalls. He may even be looking for unethical opportunities, believing that he can disregard others and do what he wants with impunity. If this type of therapist shows up ultimately before an ethics review board, he might wonder what all the fuss is about and might never understand the harm he caused his client(s). The therapist might be sorry he got caught but be no more interested in expanding his ethical consciousness than before. He might attend workshops or therapy because those are provisions for keeping his license, even though he does not see why these measures are necessary. Such remedial therapy, if it is to be successful, must first break down the therapist's denial about the choice he made to fill his own needs at the expense of his clients.

Some caregivers may even lack an ability to genuinely care about their clients. Caregivers who lack the first key to professional behavior (authentic caring) can, at best, only follow the therapeutic, legal, or ethical letter of the law. They will not be able to form right relationships or provide caring responses. These caregivers have probably not done the deep work required to uncover and deal with whatever personal wounds keep them from feeling their caring and connection to others.

Disregard for the client is especially problematic when the therapist works with clients in nonordinary states of consciousness. Many clients have issues of not being loved and not being good enough. In a nonordinary state, clients may internalize a therapist's lack of regard for them, escalating this self-blame exponentially. Diffusion of self-other boundaries in the nonordinary state, together with an increased emotional and physical sensitivity, may lead clients to blame themselves for not being worthy of full or caring attention from their therapists. They may reimprint what they learned during their own experience of emotional child abuse: that they are merely useful (to pay fees, give sexual favors, or bolster the therapist's self-esteem) but not lovable.

The second type of disregard for a client happens when caregivers unconsciously disregard clients. In this type of disregard, caregivers are usually thrown off track by caregiver burnout, ignorance of possible ethical pitfalls, or their own unexamined issues, defense mechanisms, or spiritual longings.

Caregiver burnout

Most therapists and other caregivers do not disregard their clients. They authentically care for their clients. Many caregivers on occasion, however, feel burned out. We feel we have too many clients, too much stress in our own lives, and too little recreation. Each contributes to burnout. If our lives revolve primarily around our therapeutic or ministerial work, we disproportionately come into contact with the pain of the troubling times and difficult emotions of life. We are particularly vulnerable when we pay too little attention to our own psychospiritual journeys, when we do not acknowledge ourselves as each having an "inner child" of our own, when we do not put our own spiritual practice first, and when we do not schedule time for our own growth and care.

Caregiver burnout is more relative to how many unresolved issues we have than to the number of clients on our caseload or the amount of stress indicators we tally. The computer offers a metaphor for this. If we have too many files tied up in Random Access Memory (RAM), then the computer becomes overloaded and sometimes freezes. If we unload our files (resolve our own childhood trauma, deal with our own fears, desires, and longings), then our RAM is available for quick and present response to clients.

Causes of Caregiver Burnout

- Too many clients

- Too much stress in one's life

- Not enough recreation

- Not enough attention to self care and personal psychological growth

- Not enough attention to personal spiritual path or practice

---

When therapists' own care of themselves is in deficit, they have no care available for others either. Caregiver burnout diminishes authentic caring and makes therapists vulnerable to unethical behavior. When caregivers have an inner child screaming *It's my turn!*, they cannot care for their clients in an undistracted, wholehearted manner, even if they deeply and intently care about those clients most of the time.

Particularly when planning a session of breathwork, shamanic work, or other nonordinary state work, it may be wise for a caregiver to check the level of her own reservoir of caring. Intense experiences sometimes require the client to draw large amounts from the caregiver's supply of caring to help in healing the client's own untended wounds. If a caregiver runs out of caring in the middle of such a session, he may be likely to substitute some other form of attention such as criticism, anger, or disappointment. Or, having no more caring to give, he may simply abandon the client psychically, emotionally, and energetically.

Prevention of ethical misconduct seems to involve attention to self-care. Pacing our workload, balancing our lives with recreation, self-growth, professional continuing education, and personal spiritual practice can go a long way toward allowing us to look forward to time with our clients.

Ignorance of the pitfalls

When a caregiver has never considered a possible sex, money, or power situation with a client, he is more vulnerable to falling into a course of unethical action inadvertently. It is even more likely that a caregiver has not considered the possible intense emotional, spiritual, transpersonal, or nonordinary state situations, which might result in his acting unethically. He does not recognize the impending signs in himself or the situation. He has not heard others' stories in which they relate the choices that led them down the road toward misconduct, the consequences they experienced, and how they extricated themselves from those places. The caregiver either thinks these pitfalls do not exist or that others are at risk, but he is invulnerable to falling into them.

As caregivers, we maintain a general state of ignorance in ourselves and our colleagues when we do not talk with each other about these things. We stray from the path of right relationship and then keep silent to avoid breaking the taboo preventing openness about ethical dilemmas and mistakes. We caregivers often think we should live up to some ideal of human perfection for caregivers because our peers do not talk about their mistakes and their countertransference issues. When we do hear our peers share their own experiences personally and professionally, we can empathize with their decisions and their hurtful consequences. Knowledge of the pitfalls comes firsthand, of course, when caregivers step into the pits themselves. But I do not believe the "school of hard knocks" is the only educational opportunity. There are times when discussion, reading, and self-examination actually prevent the missteps that ignorance invites.

Therapists also start thinking differently and looking before they leap after attending ethics workshops and presentations. When therapists enter into discussion with others about situations which present potential ethical dilemmas, they start to hear, see, and feel in a different way. When we hear ourselves speak aloud about these issues, we can be alerted to where we might tend to rationalize. In seeing the reaction of peers to discussion of their own issues, we can see patterns to which they might be blind. In feeling the possible consequences of acting unethically, we renew our resolve to learn to avoid this pain.

Underestimation of the power of nonordinary states of consciousness (and transference) to affect us

Caregivers know that clients' having intense experiences affects them. However, they often cannot accurately predict how much they will be influenced or even determine how much they are moved at the time they feel the effects. There is a physical transmission that is particularly palpable during nonordinary states. Energy from a person in a nonordinary state seems to circulate, find, and react with the energy in other human beings who are present. It is this principle that makes group ritual or group meditation so powerful. The emotions and energetic movement of one person triggers emotions or movement in others.

This is one of the principles behind the Network Chiropractic practice of sometimes treating several patients simultaneously in one room. The doctor moves among them from one to the other performing adjustments to spinal subluxations. Energy circulates among the patients as well. Energy circulation is also a principle in the design of a Holotropic Breathwork workshop. The energetic, visible, and audible experiences of some participants loosen tight bundles of unfinished grief, joy, anger, and compassion in other participants so that this energy can at last move and express itself.

The group structure of the two techniques above restrains unethical conduct. Everything is done within sight of others. The boundaries of the setting and the philosophy of the set is clear to everyone. There is often more than one person facilitating. In an individual session, however, a caregiver is much more likely to be swayed in some way by the client's nonordinary state. The energy of the state is powerful. The caregiver is alone with the client. There is no one else present as a reference point to ordinary consciousness. The caregiver could be catapulted suddenly into his own nonordinary state by the client's energy or the content of the client's process. The checks and balances of the group setting are missing.

A trained shamanic counselor and some massage practitioners may have learned to use a nonordinary state professionally. By keeping a foot in both worlds, the professional can feel into the client's non-ordinary space and interface for him and with him in ordinary reality. Interestingly, however, shamanic work is often done in groups also. In "individual" sessions, a well-trained shamanic practitioner often will have another person present, perhaps a drummer, to hold the contact with ordinary reality as the therapist/shaman journeys on behalf of the client.

In many cases a therapist, bodyworker, or minister is not trained specifically to work with the intense, unusual experiences described in *Chapter 2*. In moving into her own nonordinary state, the caregiver may divert her awareness from her client's process or become ineffective in responding to her client's needs. She may even react to the client's process because of her own fears or desires (countertransference). In any of these reactions—removal of awareness, inefficacy, or unacknowledged countertransference—the therapist has an impaired perspective and an ability to respond appropriately to the client's needs.

Because of this tendency of energy to affect energy, a caregiver working with clients in profound states needs, more than any other single attribute, her own extensive experience doing her own work as a client in nonordinary states of consciousness. I have seen many seasoned therapists participate in a Holotropic Breathwork workshop for the first time. Some, even those who have undergone their own extensive personal talk therapy, are astounded by the emergence of their own buried intensities. One middle-aged psychiatrist said he had completed three psychoanalytic training analyses but had never experienced such profound, rapid, and life-changing therapy as he is undergoing now by working with breathwork and shamanic techniques. Other therapists, presuming they have become jaded through hearing the many stories of clients in their offices, are surprised by their deep reactions to the emotions, experiences, and sharing of other participants in the room.

Psychiatric technicians and aides who work in in-patient facilities and hospice workers are bombarded with nonordinary states of consciousness daily. Exploring their own psyches through intense inner work (breathwork, hypnosis, etc.) might make their jobs easier and more rewarding. If we have resolved much of our own inner material, we do not need to protect ourselves from feeling it. We no longer need to erect barriers in ourselves to the client's material. Ultimately we can be present with the client—feeling his pain and not removing ourselves because of it.

Traditionally shamans, whose job descriptions define them as mediators between the everyday world and the "spirit" world, were qualified by virtue of their own experience in nonordinary states of consciousness. The intimate nature of a tribe ensured that everyone knew something of the personal ordeal of the shaman's training and its results.

In today's modern world anyone can do "shamanic work." The small community of a tribe allowed everyone to know who had done what work and how it turned out. Without the context of a tribe, it is incumbent on those who seek shamanic healing or wisdom to investigate the qualifications of shamans. Qualification is based upon the shaman's personal experience in nonordinary states of consciousness and a proven ability to meditate the experiences of others in nonordinary states. "Shamans" who have not been trained through extensive personal experience are conducting their own learning process at the expense of clients. Since it is stylish to call oneself a shaman, some people with poor boundaries, lack of self-knowledge, and unresolved self-esteem issues, who are not rigorously trained, may honor themselves with this title.

To stay naturally grounded (without need for repression or other defense mechanism) during a flood of grief, an inferno of anger, or the hurricane of elation, a therapist must have faced his own fears of emotional expression. In other words, he can personally identify with the release his client is experiencing, without fear of it. The therapist has embodied sadness, rage, and joy in his own past experiences. The therapist has faced his own fears of beginning a frightening process without a foreseeable ending. He has surrendered to intense emotions and has had his own deep experiences of risking, feeling, moving, and expressing. He has come to completion regarding some of his issues or experiences. These experiences allow him to deeply trust the flow and sequence of any process in his clients and know that ultimately the process will complete itself.

I am not advocating perfection before undertaking nonordinary state work with clients. Caregivers, even if they have had these kinds of deep experiences, will not always be comfortable with a particular client's intense experience. However, if the caregiver has had her own intense and profound experiences, she knows what interventions have been helpful or unhelpful to her. If she has had her own moment of exploration into unknown psychic territory and found a successful return from it, she is more likely to be able to transfer that confidence to her work with a client. She will trust that the client's process is benign and moving toward resolution even when it appears hopeless to the client.

Qualities of a Caregiver Experienced with Nonordinary States

- Identifies with client expression, without reacting from personal fear or need

- Knows when not to intervene

- Knows when and how to assist the process

- Trusts the process to unfold appropriately

- Trusts that the process will complete itself

- Has a teacher or community to turn to when needing assistance

---

Although caregivers often enter trance states themselves when working with a client, the trance state that the caregiver enters will not be one in which she tends to psychically disappear (dissociate) or use other defense mechanisms to retreat from being present with a client during biographical regression or transpersonal states. She will probably continue to respond, rather than react, and to provide effective support for the client.

Our unexamined personal issues (countertransference)

Chapters 5, 6, and *7* (money, sex, and power) discuss this particular vulnerability to unethical behavior in detail. When caregivers examine their personal sensitivities to these issues, they bolster their awareness and may actually prevent certain scenarios from unfolding. When caregivers identify their own defenses and stop disavowing their vulnerabilities, they can mediate more easily between their more self-serving motives and their higher values.

If a caregiver discovers he is particularly vulnerable to money issues, he can be attentive to his own fears which arise in the context of therapy. If his fears of insufficiency involve money, he can be particularly circumspect with his fee structure and in refusing clients' gifts and favors. He can seek therapy to increase his own feelings of self-esteem, expectations of abundance, and security. He can face his fears of change by taking appropriate risks. By stretching rather than contracting in his own personal process, he will communicate to his clients a courage and a trust in the process of the change itself that is therapy.

Perhaps a particular caregiver is most vulnerable to sex issues and easily enticed by sexual seduction. Knowing this, a caregiver can be alert to romantic transference and to her own fantasies about clients. She can be wary of her own rationalizations that persuade her she really does not need peer consultation about a client to whom she is attracted or that her relationship with a certain client is a special situation exempt from the usual precautions. She can take preventive steps to get her physical touching needs and romantic longings fulfilled in other ways outside of her professional associations.

A caregiver who is especially vulnerable to power issues can be vigilant about his own desires or fears related to control of himself, the client, or the client's process. He can note his own defenses about admitting such control issues and pay special attention to when he distorts his self image by devaluing himself or inflating himself unrealistically. He can seek and listen to feedback from his peers. Working as a co-therapist in a group is one way to seek accurate feedback about control issues. The two co-therapists can provide each other with objective information about the way they interact with the clients.

Defending ourselves from feeling unethical

Where we have unconscious countertransference, some part of us is defending us from knowing about it. Usually some part of us knows when we have moved off the path of right relationship. If a caregiver has made a conscious decision to act in a way which puts her own needs ahead of her client's, she may have conscious or unconscious cognitive dissonance. The conflict of cognitive dissonance occurs when part of us wants to take care of our client's needs and part of us wants to satisfy our own needs. If we act in a way that is not congruent with our values, we probably will have to defend one part of ourselves from the other part of ourselves to keep from feeling the pain of cognitive dissonance.

Say, for example, I believe I am a professional who cares about her client and is committed to *do no harm* therapeutically. At the same time, I am romantically attracted to a client and have had ambiguous eye contact with him, even while communicating verbally in a clearly professional way. I am sending double messages. But in order to keep from dealing with or even consciously knowing that I am sending double messages, I may make any number of defending moves. I may project the romantic fantasy onto my client, calling it transference. *He* is romantically attracted to *me*! I may repress it and *forget* to bring it to supervision. I may overestimate my ability to control myself and underestimate my need for professional consultation about this client. I may simply ignore the part of my double message that is romantic eye contact and believe my own professional voice when it says there is nothing unethical going on.

In another scenario, I might rationalize to myself that this client is not ready to start a relationship with someone he just met. Without conscious awareness of my jealousy, I give "therapeutic advice" to my client to wait a bit. Needless to say, my clarity dims along with my integrity when I rationalize that whatever I did was for the good of my client.

Caregivers also feel less clear when they encounter situations they have not heard about before, where they do not know their own unconscious longings, and where they are afraid to ask for consultation. The first step off an ethical standard of right relationship is at least clear and honest. *I did that!* The second step away is not. *I did not do that!* Denying the truth of what is happening is dishonest. Two steps away, the caregiver may feel less vulnerable to unethical behavior but, in fact, may be more vulnerable. If the caregiver is not willing to tell the truth to herself, she is probably invested in the course she is on—getting what she wants at the expense of the client. She does not want to know what she is doing, if knowing might mean changing her actions or strategies.

If we are willing to tell the truth to ourselves, we take a step in returning to right relationship and clarity. Caregivers who begin to ask themselves the kinds of questions that appear at the end of each of the chapters on the seven centers are engaging in honest self-examination. If someone really wants to know the truth, she is generally willing to do whatever is necessary to stay in alignment with that truth once she sifts through her defenses to find it.

Countertransference and transference in dual relationships

Most often, ethical issues pertaining to work with clients in nonordinary states are subtle. Countertransference, and especially transference, can be important to consider in relating to a client in more than one role and for one function. The needs of the client vary considerably with regard to boundaries and safety. Some clients are more flexible and at ease in moving from child to adult ego states, from mythical reality to ordinary, functional reality, and in making changes in the power balance between them and their caregivers.

Some clients grow over time through different phases of relationship with their therapists, ministers, masseuses, and teachers. Some models of caregiving are more rigid about the so-called phenomenon of *dual relationship* than others. There has been quite a bit of dialogue about what sort of dual relationship is unethical and what sort might be ethical or even therapeutic.

A dual relationship is one in which those involved have roles with each other that are not only therapeutic but social, or not only professional but personal. Lawrence E. Hedges, a supervising psychoanalyst, expresses relief that after twenty years (December 1992) the term *dual relationship* has been stricken from the American Psychological Association's (APA) code of ethics.* He says, "The faulty shift of ethical focus from *damaging exploitation* to *dual relationships* has led to widespread misunderstanding and incessant naive moralizing which has undermined the spontaneous, creative, and unique aspects of the personal relationship which is essential to the psychotherapeutic process."[117] He makes a strong point that the emphasis in ethical codes should be on preventing exploitation of clients rather than on preventing all relationships with multiple facets or on preventing the natural, healthy developmental changes that occur in relationships between caregivers and clients. A psychiatrist remembered that his psychoanalytic supervisor expected that real relationship would develop, and coincident with termination, a friendship would be in place. This was considered the ideal outcome of a successful therapy.

Caregivers and dual relationships

Models differ in the latitude they allow for dual relationships. The American Association for Marriage and Family Therapy, for example, is explicit that dual relationships, which detract from therapeutic effectiveness or which exploit clients, are unethical:

> *Marriage and family therapists . . . . therefore make every effort to avoid dual relationships with clients that could impair their professional judgment or increase the risk of exploitation. When a dual relationship cannot be avoided, therapists take appropriate professional precautions to ensure judgment is not*

---

*The current APA code does not prohibit dual or multiple relationships, but it also does not require that actual exploitation occur in order for there to be a violation of the code, only that there is an increase in risk of exploitation occurring.

impaired and no exploitation occurs. Examples of such dual relationships include, but are not limited to, business or close personal relationships with clients. Sexual intimacy is prohibited. Sexual intimacy with former clients for two years following the termination of therapy is prohibited.[118]

The American Psychological Association goes further in its instruction to members about sexual contact with former clients, stating:

. . . psychologists do not engage in sexual intimacies with former therapy patients and clients even after a two-year interval except in the most unusual circumstances. The psychologist who engages in such activities after the two years following cessation or termination of treatment bears the burden of demonstrating that there has been no exploitation, in light of all relevant factors.[119]

Another model simply prohibits dual relationships altogether:

The Registered Music Therapist shall not enter into dual relationship with clients or students and will avoid those situations which interfere with professional judgment or objectivity (e.g., competitive and conflicting interests) in their relationships.[120]

The Feminist Therapy Institute speaks of *overlapping relationships* instead of dual relationships and writes in its *Ethical Guidelines for Feminist Therapists*:

A feminist therapist recognizes the complexity and conflicting priorities inherent in multiple or overlapping relationships. The therapist accepts responsibility for monitoring such relationships to prevent potential abuse of or harm to the client.[121]

Twelve Step members and dual relationships

The Twelve Step model of caregiving allows for and even expects the development of a caregiving (sponsor) relationship into a peer relationship (friendship). Intervening to bring an addict into treatment requires a peer or family member to move into a detached role long enough to deliver a firm dose of reality, generally only possible from a professional role. Within the Twelve Step community, there is often permission for relationships to be somewhat fluid and reciprocal. Some members of Twelve Step programs are able to progress developmentally in their relationships with each other as appropriate.

Teachers and dual relationships

Teachers disagree about suitable boundaries between student and professor. Some think teachers should maintain a strict distance, others think students benefit by a more personal relationship with their teachers. Rita Manning writes:

> *We must be open to the possibility of being friends with our students. To do otherwise is to refuse to see them as complete human beings, to see them merely as students . . . . An ethic of care says that we must respond to each student as one caring. We must try to see each student in his or her particularity. This is not to say that it is easy or even possible to do this in a real classroom; the institutional barriers to meeting our students as one caring are daunting and, I fear, growing.*[122]

Clergy and dual relationships

Members of the clergy are challenged to participate in the complex interweaving of roles and personalities that, although formidable, is definitely within human capability. Curiously, this multiplicity of function is generally considered normal for ministers, while it has become perverse or questionable for psychotherapists.

Members of the clergy have to step nimbly between the myriad roles they play with their clients (church members). With many of the same people, they have social relationships, co-worker relationships, a teaching role, and a counseling function. Clergy also share with their church members a kind of peer or family identification as a congregation. In most cases this works well and clergy learn how to be flexible in relationship while living up to their parishioners' trust. A well-functioning ministerial relationship demonstrates the human potential for complex, benevolent interactions between a professional caregiver and his clients, students, or church members.

On the other hand, the multiplicity of roles may invite ethical misconduct in those who seek to abuse their power or those who are not aware of the pitfalls. Marie M. Fortune points out in her book, *Is Nothing Sacred?* that church leaders have unusually intimate access to their flock and a high degree of trust by virtue of their office. There is potential for the most serious betrayal of trust and abuse of power within the congregational family just as in the nuclear family. She notes that religious institutions have been in denial regarding ethical misconduct of their clergy. Many have thus far prepared few guidelines to help a congregation or a religious order protect itself and stop the abuse of professional clerical power if it is occurring.[123]

The family doctor and the shaman had dual relationships

The family doctor, who practiced in the small town community in which I was raised, was a friend to his patients. He relied on his patients (his community) for services of a non-medical nature. Going back into human history still further, the tribal shaman performed his healing or oracular functions while in a certain role and with a certain ritual but was fully a member of the community in other respects and at other times. Arnold Mindell, writing in *The Shaman's Body* says of his experience with a couple who were shamanic healers in Kenya: "These [were] quiet and reserved people who worked as laborers by day and as magicians by night . . . . What healed most of all was that these shamans were real people."[124]

The relationship of community to ethical behavior within dual relationships

The politically correct model described by professional psychology today seems predicated on the anonymity of and the lack of community involvement in a therapeutic relationship. People who never meet outside the therapy office do not need to learn caring flexibility. In the small communities of the church, the family doctor, the tribal shaman, or some Twelve Step fellowships, there may be a self-regulating effect from the group context. Inappropriate behavior of a member is visible, generally known, and talked about by her community. Someone who causes harm to others usually receives consequences in the form of feedback or ostracism. Gossip forewarns other community members who might otherwise be victimized by someone who acts unethically.

Perhaps the lack of community in modern times, combined with the secrecy of confidentiality laws and small private offices, requires rigid codes of conduct applied as external force. The current stance opposing dual relationship does not recognize the potential for a developmental change in the balance of power between the client and caregiver, the development of reciprocity, or the remarkable human ability to grow, adapt, and create right relationship in its many forms. Rigid thinking about dual relationship does not promote the development of an internal locus of control with regard to ethics.

Moving therapeutically from a directive to a non-directive role

In a sense, the therapeutic role in working with nonordinary states of consciousness is so different that some of the same flexibility needed for developmental changes in the therapist/client relationship may be required by both parties in moving between therapeutic work with clients in ordinary states and nonordinary state sessions. While the role of the professional or the client does not change, there are significant changes in the ways of working with a client who is having profound experiences spontaneously or because they have been induced by some technique. (See *Chapter 2*).

Possible Changes in the Therapeutic Relationship When Clients Experience Nonordinary States

■ The therapist may move from a directive to a non-directive role.

■ The boundaries of both therapist and client may diffuse in order to share transpersonal states.

■ The definition of appropriate touch may be quite different.

The therapist may move from a directive to a non-directive role. In following the process put into motion by the intensity of the client's state, the best therapeutic course is for the therapist to relinquish her ideas about direction and to follow and support the internal therapeutic direction (inner healer) as much as possible. The therapist is not transferring her authority to the client's ordinary, cognitive understanding. Rather, both client and therapist are surrendering to a wisdom greater than the conscious theory or beliefs held by either of them. Both are allowing the client's internal wisdom to move into executive control of the therapeutic process because they understand that this inner healer has the broadest view and most benevolent agenda possible.

The boundaries between client and therapist may be more diffuse

Another change may be greater permeability of personal boundaries. When the therapist is present with the client who is in a nonordinary state, she herself must be sensitive in a special way. This seems to require the therapist to identify more than she usually does with the part of herself which is one with everything and everyone. This necessitates letting down the barriers which keep the therapist's experience separate from the *other* (in this case, the client). The following passage is about the role of the sitter in breathwork workshops but can apply equally to the role of any minister, caregiver, or therapist sitting with a client in a nonordinary state:

> *The state of the sitter is akin to meditation. The relationship between someone in a nonordinary state of consciousness (the breather) and someone who is uncatalyzed, who remains grounded in ordinary consciousness (the sitter), is a sacred and delicate one. It requires a reaching of consciousness and sensitivity on the part of the sitter, an attention to nuance, and a meditation on the chasm between the two states and building a bridge to join them. The breather often senses the two-way flow of seeing and being seen, hearing and being heard, touching and feeling.*[125]

When the boundaries of both are diffused, the caregiver may feel and intuit the experience of the client. It is possible that a real psychic connection can develop in which the caregiver knows, without hearing in words, the images, feelings, historical references, and transpersonal experiences of the client.

Boundaries between the states may blur for the client and also for the caregiver. For example, in shamanic work, the hypnotic power of myth and symbolic language enables clients to reorganize and release processes of the bodymind that need healing. The blurring of boundaries between ordinary and nonordinary reality enable the powerful insight, energy, and emotion of nonordinary states to affect ordinary reality, thinking, the body, and other matter. The boundaries between realities, after all, are ones which the mind sets artificially. What is *is,* no matter if it is called ordinary or nonordinary reality.

At times, the therapist may consciously take a role in the nonordinary state experience of his client. Lawrence Hedges, a psychoanalyst whose primary work is consulting about countertransference issues, writes about shamanic work in which the client can play out a healing drama. The client does this by projecting the therapist into the role of healer/magician *for the duration of the nonordinary state*. Such a drama enacted in nonordinary states is safe only to the extent that the client and therapist have a firmly established ordinary relationship or ordinary therapeutic relationship and some history of flexibly returning to their ordinary roles. Sometimes, especially in ritual work, the nonordinary state shared by the therapist through the client's metaphors of movement and language helps the client give expression to what is otherwise inexpressible. "The transition to the verbal system makes it possible to undergo in an ordered and intelligible form an experience that would otherwise be chaotic and inexpressible."[126]

After returning to ordinary consciousness, therapist and client can discuss the temporary change in roles. The ability to switch groundrules and methods and reinstate some boundaries when the nonordinary state work is finished is a skill needed to maintain a multiplicity of functions and roles within an ethical relationship.

Hedges offers insight into the subtleties of countertransference and transference which he believes are part of the essential healing relationship. He compares psychotherapy to shamanic work and urges therapists to remember that the strength of the real (ordinary) relationship between therapist and client allows a transition between prosaic reality to myth and symbolic healing (in nonordinary consciousness).[127]

The knowledge that the therapist is a real person allows a client to enter the mythic world without becoming lost in it, unable to return. When the therapist can journey to the world of "magic" and myth and re-enter the ordinary world at the end of a session, the client can feel at a deep level that it is safe to explore unknown territory—that she can return. The therapist actually role models re-entry skills in this case. The client may feel greater trust on many levels. The client can feel *it is safe to identify with my dream imagery* or *it is safe to embark on my greater spiritual journey into the unknown.*

The definition of appropriate touch may be different

The definition of appropriate touch may be quite different with the client in a nonordinary state. Before the nonordinary state session, the caregiver and client can discuss the wishes of the client about touch in various situations that might develop. The caregiver can also convey her feelings about touching and talk about the differences in the way she uses touch in ordinary and nonordinary state sessions. (See *Chapter 6*.)

Our unacknowledged longings (countertransference) for love and spiritual connection

Longings for the unchangeable and for spiritual sex, spiritual power, love, truth, insight, and oneness can create more vulnerability to unethical behavior because spiritual connection can be a stronger motivation than any personal fears or desires. We want money, sex, and power, but our deepest need behind these personal desires may be to feel connected to all of life and to a power greater than ourselves.

This deep need often appears as spiritual materialism. People seek to fulfill their spiritual longing with some tangible acquisition of energy, such as crystals, figures of angels, books, or scriptures. "Acquiring" a client who is in the midst of the spiritual experience one longs to have might be another way to attempt to fulfill the need for this kind of energy. The chapters on money, sex, and power (*Chapters 5* through *7*) discuss the spiritual longings for the unchangeable, for regenerative energy and mystical sex, and the longing to heal and effect change. The chapters on the transpersonal centers (*Chapters 8* through *11*) discuss the spiritual longings for compassion, truth, psychic powers, mystical understanding, union and transcendence.

We often have less experience with this compelling force of spiritual longing than we do with the personal compulsions of fear and desire. Such longings are difficult to put into words and in this culture, people are reluctant to try to speak of spiritual longings.

The force of these longings can catch us completely off guard. Especially treacherous countertransference terrain involves therapy with clients in a kundalini opening, psychic opening, or shamanic opening (forms of spiritual emergency), and multiplicity (Multiple Personality Disorder or MPD).

Countertransference with a client in a kundalini opening

The kundalini type of process opens the door to all sensations and energy flows. The client's body itself expresses spontaneously its pure life energy, demonstrating the sexual and spiritual to be inextricably intertwined. In both cases, because of our universal deep attraction to and longing for the sexual and spiritual aspects of this human energy, its manifestation in another person can be almost irresistibly seductive. Therapists and spiritual leaders, even if they do not identity "kundalini" phenomena by that name, may be in a position to feel and see this energy more intimately than others and are by no means immune to it. A healthy respect for its power is a key to preventing an unfortunate situation. Caregivers should be forewarned, as part of an adequate training program, that their attraction to this energy may have considerable leverage to sway them from their own ethical principles. A caregiver who has been particularly removed from her own body and its sensations and drives may be especially vulnerable to sexual seduction. The client's process can remind her visually and energetically of the spiritual and sexual feelings the caregiver has dissociated and for which she so deeply longs.

Countertransference with a client in a psychic opening

The psychic opening type of spiritual emergence releases the floodgates of intuition. The client may spontaneously receive information about other people and archetypal truths. She may read the mind of her therapist and close family members and friends. Therapists who are fascinated by channeling, who long to receive psychic information, and who long to gain mystical understanding may be especially vulnerable to unethical behavior with this type of client. Especially if the therapist is not easily intuitive himself, he may be at risk for sexual misconduct with someone who has these abilities. If the therapist would love to see visual images but ordinarily does not he may misuse therapeutic power by "directing" or reinforcing the client's incoming visual material. For example, if the therapist were focused on sex, he might try to encourage the client to produce or talk about sexual images. If he were fascinated by violence, he might show more interest in the past life memories of war or persecution. If he were interested in mythology, he might spend more time on eliciting details of archetypal imagery.

This attraction between a therapist and a client in the middle of a psychic opening is often played out when a person with traits described as masculine or yang (one of either gender who is more developed cognitively than intuitively and is less permeable to incoming energy) has a client demonstrating an opening of the feminine or yin (intuitive, permeable). The client in this type of opening usually experiences her cognitive or masculine parts as overwhelmed temporarily by her need to reclaim the feminine. She does not wish to, or cannot, allow the new intuitive opening while simultaneously holding on to the known, cognitive, or masculine. She is often attracted to a therapist with masculine qualities who can hold the space while she dissolves her cognitive, intuitive, and sensory barriers. The therapist in turn may be attracted to the client's ability to merge and to receive energy and information.

Countertransference with a client in a shamanic opening

The shamanic opening type of spiritual emergence traditionally requires an experienced shaman to guide the client through this training period. This preparation focuses on the uses of personal and transpersonal power. It particularly requires a caregiver to have experienced some of the death/rebirth experiences which are characteristic of shamanic opening and to face his own fear and the fears his client encounters. The caregiver working with shamanic opening may be vulnerable to issues of money and power. (See *Chapters 5* and *7*.)

This kind of process tends to activate money (security or fear) issues or power issues. Some caregivers may pretend to themselves and their clients that they are more equipped to guide someone through a shamanic opening (power) than they actually are and then find themselves suddenly out of their depth. The caregiver who can call upon an experienced shamanic practitioner as a resource when working with this type of client will greatly reduce the possibility that his own fear will impede the process.

If sex issues arise in a shamanic opening, they may relate also to power issues on the part of the therapist or shaman. The therapist may feel he is transmitting energy and power to his client, exercising power over her, or demonstrating his own power through sexual contact. In contrast, therapist-initiated sex with a client in a psychic type opening is more likely to be an attempt to acquire mystical, magical, or intuitive skills through mating with a person who has them.

Countertransference with a client who is multiple

In someone who is multiple (MPD), there are usually one or more alters or personalities who have been assigned to handle sexuality. It is sometimes the case that one identity in a multiple is the one who engages in prostitution or is the one who contains the unrestrained sexual drive. When the latter type of personality appears in the office, it seems like, in Freud's terms, *id* unencumbered by *superego*. This alter may manifest generic spiritual energy by fully taking on the form of the unrestrained, vital, regenerative energy experienced as sexual energy. If the therapist is already attracted to the client, the therapist's civilized superego may be no protection when the intense sexual energy of the client awakens deep desires in the therapist to feel his own free-flowing sexuality.

Other alters of a multiple client can appear to be disincarnate entities who channel spiritual wisdom through the client. Some can call themselves demons (as in demonic possession), although Colin Ross, a psychiatrist and an expert on dissociative disorders who says he has met many such "demons," claims that right underneath the demonic energy, they are all terribly hurt little children.[128]

Desire to explore fascinating transpersonal material (*e.g.,* psychic skills and disincarnate entities) or a deep fear of it (*e.g.,* demonic possession) can take the caregiver off the track of right relationship and therapeutic interventions. Ross describes an example where he learned how indulging his own interest in this kind of material might not be in the therapeutic best interest of his client. In his wonderful book of case histories of MPD clients, *The Osirus Complex,* he writes about the lesson he learned with Jon (a male alter of the female host, Jennifer):

> *Jon's attempt to demonstrate his ESP to me was an attempt to be accepted. I should have understood this rather than being misled by my curiosity, and I should have known that the humiliation of a failed attempt would uncover the underlying humiliation he felt about . . . the childhood sexual abuse. . . . In the future she could elect to participate in any kind of ESP research she wished, without having her decisions complicate her therapy.*[129]

Other fascinating aspects of multiplicity may include unexplained electrical phenomena (*e.g.,* power surges or inoperable electrical equipment) which occur in proximity to the client.[130] If the caregiver is attracted to the client or fascinated by these phenomena and feels pulled aside from his path of right relationship, he can take preventive steps to avoid ethical misconduct. He can begin by consulting with someone who understands both multiplicity and transpersonal countertransference.

I know personally of only a few cases which reached the point of litigation because sexual relationships between caregiver and client involved the transpersonal issues described *in Chapters 8* through *11* (centers four through seven). *All* of those I know about, however, have involved clients who are multiple.

The person with multiple personality or any dissociative disorder has adopted this particular strategy to survive severe abuse in which there was no possibility of escape except into parts of oneself. The person divided responsibility for memory and functioning so that one part was not responsible for the actions of another part. The countertransference of a caregiver may likewise in some way be abusive or abdicating of responsibility. The client, a master at not taking responsibility, may also be more likely to sue.[131]

There may also be some operant principle that the degree of dissociation in the client exponentially increases the degree of risk for unethical behavior in the caregiver. Caregiver susceptibility to the issues in all seven centers, client vulnerability, and the client's subsequent anger at betrayal by the caregiver may be significantly greater when the client has suffered extreme abuse and has many alters.

Exploitation of the client as a curiosity and "case"

In each of these intense situations (kundalini phenomena, psychic opening, shamanic opening, and multiplicity), the caregiver may be intellectually as well as emotionally, physically, and spiritually intrigued. The caregiver may tend to look at the client as an oddity or as the potential subject of an interesting article. As a result, he may subtly exploit the client to satisfy his curiosity or achieve scholarly objectives. Exploitation in a therapeutic context may include asking the client questions which are relevant to research but not therapy. It may be exploitative to encourage psychic or energetic phenomena in order to satisfy a kind of spiritual voyeurism.

13

K eys to Professional Ethical Behavior

*A therapist often has the impression
that his work is going splendidly,
the deeper he falls into his own shadow.*[132]

—Adolf Guggenbühl-Craig

*T*he keys to professional ethical behavior are qualities and strategies which help us intervene with ourselves, even when we are vulnerable to unethical behavior. When we are feeling slightly off track with a client, these keys can offer us a checklist to see which key we might have neglected in a particular case.

Honor is the capacity to confer respect upon another individual. Angeles Arrien, an anthropologist and author, writes, "We become honorable when our capacities for respect are expressed and strengthened. The term respect comes from the Latin word *respicere*, which means the willingness *to look again*." [133]

Keys to Professional Ethical Behavior

■ Authentic caring

■ Willingness to examine our own motivations

■ Willingness to tell the truth

■ Willingness to ask for help (consultation) and to learn

Authentic caring

Authentic caring is action connected to the heart and to feeling. In profound states, clients are much more sensitive than in ordinary states to inauthenticity in those around them. A client often knows if a caregiver is distracted and thinking about something else while the client is reliving or emoting. The client often perceives when the therapist would rather be somewhere else than in the therapy session at the moment. The client is quick to apprehend if the therapist has a judgment about or difficulty in accepting the client's nonordinary reality.

Authentic caring for the client is the opposite of disregard for the client. I believe it is the most important component of ethical behavior. Authentic caring is not a foolproof protection against unethical behavior. A caregiver can still fool herself into believing that she is acting out of caring when she is not and that what she wants is in the client's best interests when it is not. The other keys to professional ethical behavior are important as well.

Willingness to examine our own motivations

Most of the ethical issues caregivers encounter concern the interplay between their own fears and desires (doing what they think is in their own best interests) and authentic caring (doing what is good and appropriate therapy for their clients). The interference with caring can take the form of:

> 1) Complicated, unacknowledged counter-transference or neediness (*I want what you have; I need you as a client*);
>
> 2) Simple acknowledged personal desire without an understanding of its consequences (*I want to feel I am powerful enough to have caused some of these profound effects in your life*); and
>
> 3) Powerful and unfulfilled, acknowledged or unacknowledged spiritual longings (discussed in *Chapters 5* through *11.*)

Sometimes it is fairly easy to discover our own motivations, and we do not have too much resistance to knowing the truth. For example, the motivation we uncover may be minor.

> ■ *I do not want to be here working with you right now. I would rather be home in bed with my headache.*

In this case there is no shame or guilt. The caregiver not only has a good reason (*e.g.,* headache) for doing what she wants to do, but she does not judge herself (*e.g.,* for wanting to be home instead of being at work). She has also acknowledged her distraction and has consciously chosen to continue with the session. Aware of her conflicting motives, she is able to refocus on the client.

> ■ *Yes, I should want to be here, I should not be thinking about my headache or wanting to be elsewhere, but I do not need to hide my true feelings from my-*

self. I do not feel I am a bad person because I have caught myself having this thought.

With cognitive dissonance, shame and guilt, the motivations can be more complicated and form layers so that it is difficult to get to the truth. Sometimes it is quite painful to dig and unearth one's real feelings and motivations.

■ *I am embarrassed that I am attracted to my client because of her spiritual radiance.*

■ *I do not want to admit to myself that I feel spiritually one-down because I cannot meditate every day as my client seems able to do easily.*

These layers of shame and guilt keep not only others, but ourselves, from knowing what is truly going on. Constructed to protect us from feeling bad, these layers also keep us stuck.

■ *If I am attracted to the client and I do not know it consciously, I cannot even ask for consultation.*

Caregivers' own shame and guilt probably interfere with therapeutic progress for their clients.

■ *I feel spiritually inferior whenever my client talks about her out of body experiences. My normal encouraging approach to transpersonal experiences disappears as soon as she mentions leaving her body. I am probably giving her nonverbal signals that I do not want to hear those stories. I am communicating that out of body experiences make me uncomfortable. The client may interpret my discomfort to mean that out of body experiences are uninteresting, abnormal, or even dangerous.*

A caregiver's own willingness to examine his own motivations seems to pay off also in a synchronistic willingness on the part of his clients to do the same. Most of the time, clients do not know consciously what personal issues are current for their caregivers in their caregivers' private therapy or spiritual practice. Still, a subliminal communication seems to surface. Clients seem to manifest themes, issues, resistances, and acts of courage that parallel those of their caregivers'.

> ■ *Over and over again, I have seen this synchronistic effect. When I am resistant to my next step, my clients are resistant to theirs. When I try harder to get them to take the next step, they resist harder. When I am "minding my own business" outside of my therapy sessions, taking risks, and looking deeply into my own motivations, clients are suddenly able to do the same.*

When caregivers become more caring and accepting of themselves, their clients feel more cared about and caring of themselves as well. When caregivers become more authentic, clients often do too.

Willingness to tell the truth

Willingness to tell the truth is a critical key to professional ethical behavior. Caregivers become more ethical as their willingness grows to tell the truth to themselves, to their peers, and to their clients. One of the four cornerstones of Angeles Arrien's *The Four-Fold Way* [134] is, "Tell the truth without blame or judgment." She teaches that we can, "free the field of creativity that exists within each of us by moving out of ideas of wrongdoing or rightdoing. . . . To tell the truth without blame or judgment is the capacity to say what is so."

We will discuss three kinds of willingness to tell the truth. One is willingness to tell the truth to ourselves, the second is willingness to tell the truth to our peers, and the third is willingness to tell the truth to our clients.

Telling the truth to ourselves

At some point in examining our own motivations, we become willing to tell the truth to ourselves. We can start with that willingness. We often begin by knowing that there is conflict inside and that while one part of us is willing to know, the other part is not.

■ *I am willing to know what a part of me does not want to know about my own fears, desires, and longings.*

■ *I am willing to know the truth about my motivations, even if I do not know what to do with that truth.*

■ *I am willing to know the truth about how my motivations and actions are affecting my client, even if I feel pain, embarrassment, or hopelessness.*

■ *I am ready to tell myself the truth because I hold a deep belief that the truth will set me free.*

Willingness to tell the truth to ourselves often means being ready to lay down the defense mechanisms which protect us from knowing what we are up to. A look at the specific defense mechanisms and coping styles listed in the DSM-IV[135] might provide information about which patterns we are using. Usually the DSM-IV is used to diagnose clients, but in this case, it comes in handy for diagnosing ourselves. In order to defend ourselves from the truth, we therapists use defense mechanisms, too!

Once we know that we are bolstering our denial about something, we are hot on the trail of identifying what that something is. Some of the common mechanisms we use in defending against issues with clients in nonordinary states are denial, projection, projective identification, rationalization, anticipation, dissociation, repression, humor, intellectualization, omnipotence, and devaluation.

Telling the truth to ourselves about our defense mechanisms

Denial

Denial is taking the position that what is so is not so—that what clients say they experience, for example, they really do not experience. It would be strange if most of us, as products of traditional schools and training, did not revert to this method, at times, when we face new information. We tend to do this when the new information conflicts with our belief systems or when we observe clients having experiences that we have not had ourselves.

For example, it took many years before caregivers could hear the truth and the pain of childhood incest, validate it, and bring the issue to public attention. Prior to that incest was selectively denied. Caregivers believed some of the clients' experiences but not their experience of molestation. Even now, we can use denial to keep from feeling the full emotional impact when a client relives horrific abuse or even unabashed ecstasy.

- *There is no such thing as ritual abuse in this modern age and in this community, or I would have heard about it before.*

- *Even though she says she is feeling one with everything, I think anybody who feels so elated must be manic.*

- *She says she is feeling spiritual ecstasy, but this looks more like a breakdown than any religious experience with which I am familiar.*

Denial is also ignoring our own fears and wishes or taking the position that we are beyond having such petty wants and aversions. Many of these personal and spiritual fears and desires have been discussed earlier in *Chapters 5* through *11*.

Projection

Projection is the false attribution of our own unacceptable feelings, impulses, or thoughts onto another. A caregiver might project her own attraction onto a client. A caregiver might be sexually attracted to a client whose energy is working in the fourth center (love). This client is feeling a transpersonal love *(agape)* but the caregiver, in denial about his own attraction *(eros)* to the client, might attribute his own personal love and lust to the client.

His projection is a defense against knowing he is attracted to doing something that would be unethical.

■ *The client is talking a lot about love. I believe she has a crush on me.*

Projective Identification

Projective Identification is quite likely to happen in nonordinary state sessions. If the caregiver does project his own physical attraction onto the client, the client (as described above), who may actually be in the midst of a fourth center love experience, may be subtly or directly persuaded that she is attracted to the caregiver in that more sexual, physical (second center) way.

The caregiver can also transfer fear in projective identification. For example, the caregiver can project her own fear of malevolent spirits. The client, who previously had never thought of his spirit guides as anything other than benign, might begin to fear going into these kinds of states where he might contact such evil beings. The caregiver could project such fear in a question like this:

■ *Do you ever feel your spirit guides are going to hurt you?*

Rationalization

Rationalization is occurring when a caregiver knows what she is doing but conceals her own motivations for doing so from herself. We are tempted to rationalize when we perceive our own motivations as insufficient, unethical, or self-serving. Rationalization, if it works, allows us to do what we want to do without guilt. If we knew our true motivations, we would either stop, or would feel guilty. If we stopped those particular actions, we would not get what we wanted. If we did not stop, we would make ourselves feel guilty unless we could give ourselves another reason for our behavior. Here is one rationalization.

■ *It is okay to have a sexual relationship with this client because she received psychic information that our relationship was meant to be.*

Anticipation

Anticipation can be used to second guess the client's process as a way to attempt to control it. We might also use anticipation to control our own image of ourselves as "good" therapists. Anticipation is a useful way to prepare for any eventuality. When it is done in excess, however, or as a defense against letting the process unfold as it will, it is a clue that we fear losing control. Here, the therapist anticipates the next emotion the client will feel, even though in nonordinary states, the next emotion could be rage, sadness, compassion, *etc.*

■ *What you are probably going to experience next is fear because there is always fear underneath anger.*

Dissociation

Dissociation is quite common for those sitting with someone in intense sessions. As soon as some issue is triggered in us and we cannot stay present with it, we may dissociate. Anger, grief, intimacy, touch, and even joy are likely to touch off our dissociative mechanisms. The fact that we are trying to refrain from going into process ourselves as we sit with someone may even contribute to our need to dissociate.

■ *My partner in breathwork asked to be held. She was sobbing like a three-year-old child. I held her but after a while realized I had been dissociating. It was too difficult for me to stay present with the intimate situation and my partner's powerful feelings.*

Another kind of dissociation is when caregivers gravitate to the nonordinary state because it is more attractive than the current ordinary reality they are experiencing.

■ *A phone volunteer on the Spiritual Emergence Net-*
work information and referral line says she has to be
alert in talking to callers in nonordinary states of
consciousness. Sometimes their worlds and world-
views are so captivating that she has to pull herself
back from entering those realities too.

Repression

Repression is another way to cover up material that is trying
to emerge. Caregivers often do not know what material they are
squelching or why they are doing it. Repression may allow our
feelings to surface in such a way that they seem unconnected to
cognitive material which may be too difficult to integrate. After
sitting for someone who has gone through an intense or profound
experience, we may have vague body symptoms or primal feelings
that are difficult to name. We may be repressing material that is
"half-out" and needs to be expressed as soon as we can make time
to explore inside ourselves.

Suppression

Any of the issues of the seven centers are candidates for repression. Suppression is more conscious than repression. It usually
involves a conscious or semi-conscious choice to postpone and
subdue material until there is an appropriate venue for its expression. The more experience we as therapists have in doing processes ourselves, such as breathwork, EMDR, hypnosis, *etc.*, the
more we will be able to use suppression skillfully. On those occasions when we feel a client's process is triggering our own, we can
use suppression so that, while empathizing with our client's experience, we postpone our own full-blown, similar process.

■ *I feel agitated and I have a knot in my stomach after*
this session. I remember suppressing my own process
when the client got in touch with her abuse at age
two. I need to take some time out and work with this.

Intellectualization

Intellectualization takes us out of our feelings and gives us a sense of control. We can feel (erroneously) that we know what this process is all about and why it is happening. Intellectualization can defend us against not knowing what will happen next. It can distract us from assisting the client to allow that silent, pregnant moment in therapy to bear new, unexpected fruit. Just when the client is sinking into really feeling sad about the lack of intimacy in her friendships, the therapist might intellectualize:

■ *Do you remember the time you re-experienced your birth and felt so alone in the incubator? Do you think this is why you cannot feel close to your friend?*

Bringing nonverbal emotion too quickly into cognitive expression can be another form of intellectualization. Use of this defense mechanism could signal that the therapist is uncomfortable with the client's emotions, sensations, or intuition. The degree of need that a therapist feels to interpret what is happening in the relationship—to the client, to herself, or to her peers—may also be a clue that this defense mechanism is operating.

Omnipotence

Omnipotence and devaluation are two sides of the same coin. Omnipotence was discussed in *Chapter 7* on power. As therapists we might take on some form of the role of Magician. As a defense mechanism, omnipotence may protect us from feeling the part of creation that is chaos and is out of our control. It may defend us from feelings of inferiority, fears of having no effect, and doubts about our therapeutic competence.

■ *The client has come to me because I can heal her. I know exactly what she needs!*

Devaluation

Devaluation may protect us as caregivers from adequately evaluating our contribution to our clients' processes and from our own fears of misusing spiritual power. If we believe our influence is insignificant, our potential for negative effect must also be insignificant. Devaluation can protect us from our own fear of doing harm. Devaluation can also work as a defense against expanding our world view. When we encounter a client's authentic experience that does not fit into our own paradigm, we may be frightened of enlarging that paradigm. Devaluation of the client's experience is an effective defense mechanism.

■ *The client says she has power animals and spirit guides. She is delusional.*

■ *The client says she is questioning the meaning of life. She is just depressed.*

I do not wish to imply that any of these defense mechanisms are bad or that we should not use them under certain circumstances. What I am advocating is a willingness to explore and reflect the truth to ourselves. If I use suppression consciously in order to postpone my own work until I have finished with the client's session, that may be quite appropriate.

■ *My client is expressing a lot of grief in this session. She has put me in touch with my own unexpressed grief from when my grandmother died. I can suppress it for now, if I commit to myself to create a place to allow myself to really feel this sadness within the next few days.*

Humor

Humor can be used to deflect intimacy. We use it to distract ourselves from making a deep connection within or between each other because closeness is frightening. We can use humor to break uncomfortable silences in a client session. We can use humor to attempt to tame the sometimes chaotic, horrible feelings of existential issues.

We might also use humor consciously to diffuse some of the client's attachment to us. If the client continues to feel that his experience is being honored, this might be a gentle way to restate our boundaries.

Telling the truth to our peers

The second part of the willingness to tell the truth is willingness to tell the truth to peers. Sometimes telling the truth to ourselves is not enough. We may be unable by ourselves to uncover some truth in ourselves. Something may have stalled in the therapeutic progress with a particular client. We may be groping to find our own contribution to that stuck point. Then we must get through not only our own denial and unwillingness to know, but face any unwillingness to have others know.

There are two payoffs to telling the truth to peers. One is that this is the way to get help in getting to the bottom of whatever is troubling about a therapy situation. We get to unmask our shame and then talk acceptingly and pragmatically about our motivations and actions that may be moving us into unethical territory.

The second payoff is that we begin to break the professional taboo preventing openness about ethical issues. The paradox of this secrecy is that therapists are supposed to be perfect therapists without ever failing. Teachers are supposed to be wise teachers without ever learning. Members of the clergy are supposed to become spiritual ministers to the fragility of the human condition without ever feeling vulnerable. By telling the truth to professional peers, we disarm those who perpetuate unethical activity by holding up an unrealistic goal of perfection. By revealing our own imperfections, we offer hope and humor to colleagues who are grappling with their own secrets.

Many falls into the pit of unethical behavior occur because the one who is strolling along pursuing his massage or therapy practice or his ministry is completely ignorant of any pit. He knows some of the obvious ethical problems but has not considered the subtle or energetic effects of nonordinary states. He thinks he would never have sex with a client but neither has he encountered the temptation of a mystical union with such phenomena as shared past life imagery and mutual mind reading. There have been many times when the talk among a group of practitioners or therapists has turned to an ethical dilemma involving transpersonal or nonordinary state phenomena when several people have said, *Oh, I never thought of that!*

Continuum of Difficulty in Sharing with Peers about Our Own Unethical Situations					
Easier to share.......... More difficult share					
Past Situations in which we were tempted to act unethically but did not	Past situations in which we acted unethically but learned our lesson without diffiuclt consequences	Past situations in which we acted unethically and suffered difficult consequences	Future situations in which we feel we could be vulnerable to ethical misconduct	Current situations in which we are vulnerable to acting unethically and are seeking preventative help	Current situations in which we have already acted unethically and are seeking corrective help

Sharing what we have learned collectively may eliminate most of the falls into ethical pits which occur from ignorance. It will not eliminate the falls by those people who have to learn by falling, by those who willfully disregard the signposts, or by those who want what they want at the expense of others. But I am convinced (or I would not have written this book) that when we point out the pitfalls we have fallen into, our colleagues will look closer and think more than twice before following us.

Talking about unethical experiences that are in the past

Where can professionals start to break the taboo preventing openness about ethical issues? There seems to be a continuum of difficulty in sharing our own ethical dilemmas with peers. Some are easier; some are harder. Perhaps easiest are those instances where we almost got into trouble in the past.

■ *Ten years ago I almost dated an intern whom I was supervising, but luckily my friend grabbed me by the collar and made me see what might happen, so I did not.*

Although this is not a big revelation, it does uncover the unwritten ideal of human perfection for therapists. It is worth saying aloud because it is the truth and because others who hear it may feel braver about saying their truth. It also alerts those who might not have thought they could harm the mentoring relationship in this way.

Next in difficulty might be to share an instance in the past in which we feel we actually acted unethically, but we somehow avoided a terrible consequence and learned an important lesson.

A woman therapist who had years of experience in practice tells her story of a time her personal desire skewed the therapy with a male client.

■ *The client gave me a beautiful bracelet. He had come for therapy very depressed and alienated from his feelings. As therapy progressed, he began to express tenderness more freely to his friends and family. He gloried in becoming able to talk about his attraction for me. (I had explained that we would not act on this.) He said he wanted a partner just like me. The bracelet was the first gift I had ever received from a client which really suited my taste. It was also clearly the most expensive.*

"I don't think I can accept this," I told him, though I couldn't help exclaiming over its beauty. "You have no choice," he beamed. "This is my birthday and I get to do what I want." Because I wanted the bracelet so much, I accepted it even though doing so did not feel right to me.

In the following session, I noticed that it took me about half an hour of inner struggle to move from the position of a woman being courted, back into therapist mode. Some weeks later, the client casually suggested that we go out for lunch sometime when he was my last client of the day. "Thank you for the invitation," I replied, "but I don't think it would be good for your therapy for it to get confused with a social relationship." He accepted this and continued with therapy, but I still think it would have been better if we had talked about what was going on for him in offering the bracelet, and if I had not accepted it.

Talking about our vulnerability to future pitfalls

Sharing an example of how we might be vulnerable to an ethical pitfall in the future might be more difficult. Such an admission alerts our peers, who might then be able to caution us if we took some missteps.

■ *I am studying the teachings of Edgar Cayce. I have a secret desire to channel such information also, in order to have the respect and the money that would come and to feel "special." I think because of this, I would be particularly vulnerable to unethical behavior if I were working with a client who was having a psychic opening and receiving lots of information. I might be jealous or I might want to control her process so that I could feel as if I were somehow "helping" her channel.*

Talking about unethical behavior that is current

The most courageous examples of truth-telling are when the situation is current. We are vulnerable right here and now—either we are teetering on the brink of a pitfall or we are currently in the pit, in great jeopardy and have not found a way out. Here is an example of precarious brinksmanship:

■ *Whenever my client is on the massage table, there is so much energy between us. Her body moves spontaneously wherever I touch it. She says she could never trust anyone with her body as much as me. I have told her that I have never experienced such spiritual energy with anyone before. She knows what I am thinking anyway. I think we may be soul mates. I know I should not have a relationship with a client, but this is different!*

Talking about this with another person, or preferably with a group of peers, helps break the spell. The therapist, as so often happens, has entered a nonordinary state along with this client. The physical and spiritual energies, the adoration of the client, and the feeling of power over the client's process are powerful forces capable of catalyzing a lingering nonordinary state. The therapist can benefit from bringing the basic truth of the nonordinary state work (the energy feels spiritual and the client feels special to her) to a peer group setting. There the therapist can get help in exploring her own motivations and in foreseeing consequences to various possible actions in this case.

What if the unethical action has already occurred?

■ *The therapist has told a client that she has a karmic connection to her and that she must continue therapy with her because of that past-life tie.*

■ *The therapist has advised a client to whom he is sexually attracted not to date someone else. He has told the client that her spiritual work with the therapist requires all her energy and she should not distract herself with a romantic relationship right now.*

■ *The therapist hopefully let her client know that she really wanted to go to a special workshop on kundalini which is being held in another country but that she could not afford it. The client, who is in the middle of a kundalini process and is very wealthy, has*

*offered to pay the therapist's way, saying, "I can af-
ford it. Take this as a gift! It will help you to help me!"*

■ *The therapist has had sexual contact with the client
during the client's nonordinary state of consciousness experience two months ago, but they have not
discussed it since. In fact, the client does not seem to
be talking as much as before to the therapist about
anything in her life!*

Telling the truth to clients

This brings us to the third part of willingness to tell the
truth—the willingness to tell the truth to clients. What truths do
we tell clients and how do we do it? Should we tell clients when
we are attracted to them? Should we apologize for unethical motivations when we realize we have them, but have not acted upon
them? What do clients need to hear? Would some truths be detri-
mental to tell? The Feminist Therapy Institute includes in its Ethical Guidelines:

■ *A feminist therapist discloses information to the client which facilitates the therapeutic process. The
therapist is responsible for using self-disclosure with
purpose and discretion in the interests of the
client.*[136]

Adolf Guggenbühl-Craig writes that if a client realizes a
shadow part of the therapist, it is necessary for further progress in
therapy for the therapist to admit, even painfully, to his shortcom-
ings. He cautions:

*The patient, after all, must also face painful insights.
By constantly trying to spot the workings of our psychotherapeutic shadow, to catch it red-handed, we help
our patients in their own confrontations with the dark
brother. If we fail to do this, all the patient learns
from us is how to fool himself and the world, and the
value of the analysis becomes highly questionable.*[137]

Self-Reflective Questions Regarding Truth-Telling to a Client

■ Can you tell this truth in the context of authentic caring?

■ Is there some untruth or truth (perhaps a secret) that stands in the way of clarity in the therapeutic relationship?

■ Could you be more clear and consistent when you make and keep agreements with clients?

■ When would you reveal something of your own process or vulnerabilities to your clients? How would you do it?

■ What truth do you need to tell to someone other than your client?

Willingness to ask for help (consultation) and to learn

Willingness to ask for help through prayer and meditation

Many times we can observe and change our own behavior. Other times we feel confused and stuck. If a caregiver has a spiritual orientation of some kind, this may be a place to ask for and receive help. When we put our longings in the form of prayer, they become stronger. Our fears and resistances often become weaker until we find ourselves wholeheartedly wishing for what we are praying. The longings to free ourselves from ignorance and not to do harm or create unpleasant consequences to others are prayers in themselves. Giving those prayers some ritual support, verbal expression, and time to be felt often results in insights, understanding, or creative ideas. Marianne Williamson calls prayer "the ex-

perience of words that takes us to a state beyond words: grace."[138]
Prayer can also bring problems into a state of grace or resolution.

We could use private prayer, however, as a way to avoid breaking the taboo against openness. We could use it as a way to keep from admitting that we have not been able to achieve the ideal of therapist perfection. If we are approaching or already immersed in an ethical dilemma, we might consider the benefit of adding consultation with peers to solitary prayer activity.

Willingness to ask for help through consultation with peers

Peers are other caregivers in our own profession who have experience working with clients having profound experiences in nonordinary states of consciousness. In other words, they have the background to understand the subtleties of a situation. The most valuable peers with whom to seek consultation are those who would not pull any punches because of friendship or because of favors owed. They are people who feel equal in a professional way and whose experience and advice we respect.

Choosing a Consultant

■ To whom would you go if you had countertransference issues?

■ With whom would you talk if you had already acted unethically?

■ Whom would you want to invite to join with you in a peer supervision group?

■ What qualities do these people have that make them desirable consultants?

We would seek consultation with a peer we trust to help us and not harm us. Peers can often see what their fellow professionals do not see because the peers are not deeply involved in counter-transference or transference issues with the same clients. Peers can empathize with the feelings involved in many therapeutic situations because they have had the same ones at times while working with their own clients.

Questions We Might Ask a Peer Who Consults with Us about Personal Ethical Conduct

■ What does it feel like in the situation?

■ When did you first notice you were about to act unethically?

■ How do you imagine you moved toward unethical action after you noticed?

■ What could you have done differently after you noticed the situation to avoid actually acting unethically?

■ What are your options at this point?

■ How would you feel in taking each of these options?

■ How would you feel *after* taking each of these options?

■ What do you need to tell yourself about this situation?

■ What do you need to tell your peers about this situation?

■ What do you need to tell your client about this situation?

Finding a strong, wise consultant

Can you imagine to whom you would go for consultation if you had countertransference that you felt might lead you into unethical behavior? Where would you go to talk about some unethical action that you had already done? Would you go to the same person for assistance with an action you might take as for one you had already taken? If you wanted to form a peer supervision group to talk about ethical issues, whom would you invite to join?

Perhaps, in the future, someone will come to you for help with an ethical issue. How can a peer consultant or a peer supervision group help someone who has fallen into the pit of an ethical problem and is looking for a way out? (See questions on previous page.)

Willingness to learn from experiential work in nonordinary states

Another way to ask for help and learn is to seek training. The training of the foremost importance is the one in which the caregiver experiences nonordinary state sessions herself. The wisdom that comes through to us in nonordinary states of consciousness is the best teacher of ethics. Guggenbühl-Craig writes:

> *The therapist must expose himself to something which touches him deeply, something un-analytical . . . which repeatedly throws him off balance, stimulates him, shows him time and again who he is, how weak and pompous, how vain and narrow.*[139] *Only something non-analytical can occasionally break through this resistance. The psychotherapist must be challenged by something which cannot be either mastered or fended off by his analytical weapons and techniques.*[140]

Many nonordinary state experiences produce a sensitivity to our connection or oneness with life and with the *other*—whatever or whomever the other might be. There is a deepening of respect, an honoring of ourselves and the other, and a heartfelt connection that together are at the core of ethics.

Willingness to learn from training and role-playing

Other workshops and seminars can provide us, as caregivers, with didactic information we need to avoid pitfalls we would fall into simply out of ignorance. Most valuable are classes and workshops that include exercises in which we discuss our vulnerabilities, role-play various scenarios in client sessions, or practice consulting with each other. In participating in such a workshop, we are again breaking the taboo which prevents openness about ethical issues. Professionals and students who are sharing together about ethical misconduct and unethical motivations, acknowledge that they want to forgive themselves for not achieving the ideal of the perfect helping professional.

Willingness to learn from peer supervision groups

Forming a peer supervision group that focuses on ethical issues is one affordable and pleasurable way to provide ourselves with continuing ethical education. Attending such a group regularly keeps ethical issues highlighted as the caregiver cares for clients. It is also a way for us to get to know and trust other professionals who work with or induce these powerful experiences. Then, if one of the group should have a sensitive ethical issue arise, she would feel comfortable sharing it with several trusted consultants.

The aftermath of ethical misconduct

After he has learned from unethical conduct, a caregiver may still have amends to make. Ethical extraction from unethical actions requires truth, caring, and skill. A good result needs luck as well. The caregiver might do well to consult with a peer who understands the transpersonal subtleties as well as the legal implications at hand. If there are legal risks and licensing consequences involved, an individual consultation could protect confidentiality in a way that group consultation could not. Even so, group consultation with trusted peers is probably the strongest way to face the truth and begin again with deeper self-knowledge and better preparation for authentic client caring.

Strategies for preventing misconduct

Besides the keys to professional ethical behavior, there are specific strategies for us to consider if we feel vulnerable to unethical behavior because of our spiritual longings. We can acknowledge these longings and begin to take steps along our own spiritual paths. Perhaps we can renew our commitment to daily meditation practice or prayer. Maybe we can schedule some sessions of our own using breathwork, transpersonal hypnotherapy, or shamanic journeying to strengthen our own connection to our inner spiritual life. The course of action which would most likely result in unethical behavior would be for us to try to tough it out, attempt to control the situation, use the various defense mechanisms, and stay isolated and in secrecy about both our feelings and the situation. Conversely, talking about the situation, getting therapy, and focusing on our own spiritual growth could help us move closer to fulfilling our real spiritual longings rather than finding an unethical and ultimately unsatisfactory substitute.

14

Expanding Ethical Consciousness in Community

We all jointly hold a responsibility
to create an environment of integrity.

—Jack Kornfield

Incentives for ethical community

The incentives are increasing for expanding ethical awareness in our various therapeutic or spiritual communities. The incentives include both punitive consequences and positive inducements.

Punitive consequences as incentives

The topic of ethics often arises because of the threat of punitive consequences. Individual caregivers, professional schools of therapy and massage, and churches feel the danger of legal and public relations problems. When there is an ethical issue having to do with the transpersonal centers (*i.e.,* love, truth, insight, or oneness), a client will probably translate her grievance into language that will enable her to seek legal satisfaction (*i.e.,* money, sex, or power).

The Board of Behavioral Sciences in California disciplines therapists licensed as Marriage, Family, and Child Counselors, Clinical Social Workers, Psychologists, and registered interns in these professions for criminal or unethical behavior in a professional context. Disciplinary actions by the Board are published in the magazine, *The California therapist.* I tallied the stated reasons given by the Board in each case (93 cases) during a one year period. I could categorize 79% of the actions as unethical actions in the areas of money, sex, and power. Sexual misconduct was a reason for action in 52% of the total cases. Violations of other professional ethics and various regulations accounted for 21% of actions.[141]

These statistics show that, in California at least, violation of the ethical code of professional conduct related to sex was the most likely violation to result in loss or suspension of one's license to practice therapy. Over the past twenty years, feminism has made our society acutely aware of the prevalence and the conditions of sexual abuse. Although there is always more that we can do to prevent sexual abuse, we generally know the issues and the consequences of abusing our power in this way over children, spouses, elders, employees, and therapy clients. Those who still choose to do these things generally do not do so any longer out of ignorance but out of compulsion and unhealed issues of their own.

Unethical actions involving money and power did not appear as frequently in this list of disciplinary actions. Perhaps issues with money are rarely seen as unethical until they are illegal.

Fraud, for example, accounted for half the money issues I counted. The rest included instances of borrowing money from a client, giving money to a client, and employing a client. Interestingly, in most of these cases, there was some other salient unethical act, such as sexual misconduct, criminal behavior, or infraction of a regulation, which also brought the case to the attention of the Board.

In a random survey of 1000 marriage and family counselors, surveyors studied how closely family therapists were adhering to the professional code of ethics for therapists. Some of the larger gaps between the code and actual practice were as follows. More than 85% of therapists at least sometimes accepted gifts worth more than $5 from their clients. Sixteen percent of therapists surveyed still were sometimes becoming sexually involved with an ex-client within two years of termination.[142]

My guess is that most unethical actions pertaining to the big three areas of money, sex, and power are never self-examined, never reported, never resolved, and often repeated by the same caregivers. Moreover, there is no information available yet that would indicate which of these cases involved transpersonal experiences, nonordinary states of consciousness, or compelling spiritual longings and spiritual fears.

If there is ethical misconduct in subtle, transpersonal areas of the client/therapist relationship, there may well be misconduct in the money, sex, and power arenas also. For example:

■ *A client who was diagnosed as a multiple personality sued her therapist for sexual misconduct after the two fell in love after many years of therapy and then out of love. They fell in love because of the client's profound transpersonal experiences during therapeutic sessions. This client's greatest outrage was the grievous harm she felt the therapist had done to her spiritually. This former client pursued her case relentlessly until the therapist had lost license, certification, and all her money.*

I suspect that when a therapist's spiritual longings and fears are involved in ethical misconduct, a client feels more deeply betrayed than if the therapist were motivated by simple greed or lust.

There are personal, internal consequences for ethical misconduct as well. Some negative consequences may be shame, low self esteem, fear of being discovered, and guilt about harming another human being.

Positive inducements as incentives

Some of the positive inducements for us as caregivers to expand our ethical consciousness are greater self-knowledge, more ease in discussing cases and issues with other therapists, increasing therapeutic skills to benefit clients, and a growing ability to circumvent more of the unpleasant, unethical pitfalls. Organizations benefit from increasing the reputation their practitioners have for ethical, conscious practice. When organizations consider ethical issues and quagmires in advance, they have already done prevention work. They are also then in a better position to respond to unethical actions on the part of their members, if such situations should arise.

Incentives for Expanding Ethical Awareness

■ Avoiding potential legal problems

■ Avoiding potential public relations problems

■ Seeking greater self-knowledge

■ Increasing therapeutic skills

■ Increasing skills to avoid unethical actions

■ Increasing ability to help others avoid unethical actions

Truth-telling and organizational integrity

The practice of truth-telling is one of the keys to professional ethical behavior. One way an organization can support truth-telling is to avoid using criticism or punishment to enforce the taboo preventing openness about ethical misconduct. If the community believes that increasing self-awareness prevents ethical misconduct, it must support open self-reflection. If an organization wants members to talk openly about their vulnerability to present or future unethical actions, the organization has to establish a climate in which it is safe to do so.

In addition to refraining from negative response, the organization can respond positively to truth-telling. Truth-telling becomes a norm in a culture when people feel not only that they will not be unduly punished when they tell the truth, but also that they will
be honored for saying what is so. Individuals in the community who hear a vulnerable admission about present or future actions can support it positively, saying things like:

■ *I really admire your courage (or self-insight, honesty, willingness to ask for help, willingness to change, caring about your client).*

■ *Your talking about this just now has made me realize I have some of the same issues.*

■ *You really became clear by talking about this. I am so glad because now you will have a chance to avoid all the mess you could have gotten into.*

An organization can actively encourage members to give feedback to each other directly by writing this value into its codes and mission statements. Here is one such example:

■ *We subscribe to the value of self-examination in order to promote personal growth in ethics. Because practitioners who keep these [Ethical] Agreements avoid behavior which may be exploitative to partici-*

pants and may also bring injury to the larger Holo-
tropic Breathwork community, we subscribe to the
principle that we need to give and receive feedback
from each other.[143]

The members of the community can practice telling the truth directly. Individuals in the community can refrain from talking about another member's ethics behind his back. Instead, we can talk to him directly about what he is doing, how it is affecting him (or his clients), and what he can do to change his behavior.

■   *If a teacher's ethical conduct is questioned, then*
members of the community who are concerned are
requested to go directly to that teacher to discuss and
try to solve the difficulty.[144]

How an Organization or a Community Can Support Truth-Telling

■   Avoid criticizing or punishing someone who breaks the taboo against openness about unethical conduct

■   Respond positively to truth-telling

■   Encourage members to give feedback to each other

■   Tell the truth directly

Talking to someone directly is not the norm in this society. We feel that if we have a problem with someone's behavior, she will not like us. Furthermore, she may not change her behavior either. The person who hears the feedback is at first often defensive and may indeed feel the person giving the feedback must not like her. The giver of feedback may fear he will be harmed in some way in retaliation. These fears may be quite realistic. Support from within or without the community can be crucial in allowing constructive confrontation to happen.

It is difficult to change a large society's way of dealing with these things. We are so used to depending on some "authority" to deal with the unethical actions of other people, even when they affect us. In our smaller communities, however, we can begin to make it the norm to take personal responsibility for what we see and what we feel. This ownership of group integrity is crucial to creating ethical community. Personal, responsible action often means telling the truth directly. Such direct truth-telling requires several conditions.

Loving support for the person getting feedback

We usually will not accept and consider constructive criticism without feeling that the one giving feedback sincerely cares about us. When we do not feel cared about, our walls go up. It helps if the person who has feedback for us can remind us about the caring nature of the feedback. The person telling his truth can have the feeling of authentic, loving support, even if he is angry.

■ *I care about you. I am angry with you. I want you to hear what I have to say. If you think there is something to what I tell you, I would like to work together with you to do something about it.*

Agreement to listen to the feedback

Talking about process before we discuss content will help clarify the motivations of the giver of feedback. It also allows the recipient of the feedback some choice. In other words, *tell the person what kind of thing you want to tell her and how you want to tell her, before you* tell *her.* When she knows there is something coming, she may need a little time to prepare herself to hear it. She may want to get some support from a third party while she hears it. In any case, she will be agreeing to hear it. She will not receive unsolicited feedback or even receive solicited feedback at a time or in a place when she cannot hear it.

■ *There is something about which I want to talk to you. It has been bothering me and I have been tempted to*

talk to other people about it, but if I were you, I would
want to hear about it directly from me. Can I talk to
you about it? If so, when and where can we do that?

Describing the behavior

In talking about the unethical behavior, the person giving the feedback can take care not to indict the character of the person, but to explain how his behavior appears to be unethical.

■ *I do not believe you are an unethical person. How-*
ever, here is the way I believe you have gone off the
track. . . .

■ *I would not even be talking about this with you if I*
didn't like and support you as a person. It is this
particular behavior that I want you to consider
changing. Here are my reasons . . . .

The person giving feedback can make as clear a statement as possible about what he saw, heard, or sensed. He can explain how this behavior seemed to be off the track of right relationship.

■ *In the massage class, I saw your body touch the client's*
genitals. I sensed she was aroused and uncomfortable
about it.

■ *I heard from three different clients of yours that you*
did hypnotic past-life regressions with them and
asked all three of them about their sexual history in
those lives.

Willingness to talk about one's own feelings

After presenting the facts, the person giving feedback can say how he feels about the situation. This does several things. It engages the truth-teller with his own feelings. He is not just pointing the finger outwards, he is checking in with himself and sharing honestly what is there. It demonstrates that the behavior has affected someone and that the behavior might have consequences. It also puts the person who is receiving the feedback in touch with possible consequences to his behavior. Here are some ways to express feelings while talking to someone about unethical behaviors:

■ *I am afraid that you will not like me anymore if I tell you this.*

■ *I feel worried that if you continue this behavior and others see me associating with you that they will think I condone this behavior.*

■ *I fear that there will be consequences for our community if you continue this behavior.*

■ *I am angry at you for putting yourself, your client, and all of us in jeopardy.*

Asking for a change in behavior

The person giving feedback can tell the other what he would like to see changed about the behavior. He may want it to stop. He may simply want to make the other person aware of a potentially unethical situation. He can also offer suggestions to the other about getting consultation or therapy.

■ *I want you to be careful not to touch the client's genitals in doing future massages.*

■ *It seems to me that to ask three clients about their sexual histories in past lives when they have not given any indication that this is relevant to them is not therapeutic. It actually seems invasive to me. If this is true, I want you to stop doing it.*

Willingness to follow up

The last requirement in truth-telling to our peers is a willingness to follow-up. The person giving feedback can provide consultation referrals and check back to see how the other is doing with the issue or the client. This communicates both caring and commitment to following through on the concern. There may be additional action needed, such as setting up a mediation or involving the greater community in some way.

■ *How can we follow up on this? I would like to check back with you in a week to see how you are feeling about this and what has happened. If you have any other thoughts after this meeting, please call me before then.*

Recipe for Direct Truth-Telling

■ A sense of support and encouragement in speaking up

■ A feeling of authentic, loving support for the person to whom you give feedback

■ Agreement from the person that the person will hear the feedback

■ An ability to separate the behavior of the person from that person's character or identity

■ A clear statement describing the unethical behavior

■ A willingness to talk about your own feelings in regard to the matter

■ A clear statement describing what you would like to see changed, worked on, or discussed

■ Willingness to follow up on the situation

"Leader of a movement" syndrome

Spiritual leaders and developers of new therapy techniques are particularly at risk to unethical behavior because they often lack peer feedback and supervision. Many have created situations which ensure insulation from teachers or peers and dependence on students. Students, because they have less power than their teacher, feel they cannot tell him the truth. Even if they can present their opinions, they are his students. Many teachers are not inclined to learn from their students, especially about their own ethical misconduct. Most of the leaders who have been the subjects of well-publicized, unethical behavior have been men, although women are not immune from these vulnerabilities.

> ■ *A therapist may isolate himself from colleagues who are genuine peers or mentors. He sees himself as a pioneer in his field, a maverick, a creative genius who is ahead of his time. His peers present him with ethical objections to his treatment of family, friends, lovers, students, and clients, but he dismisses this feedback as the moralistic grumbling of smaller, "neurotic" minds, jealous of his attainments and his following.* [145]

This therapist or spiritual leader is often the founder of his own school of therapy or spiritual center. He may set up a lifestyle in which his only intimates are those in awe of him. From them, he may at times accept feedback about his ethics if the feedback is presented hesitantly for his consideration and does not threaten anything he really wants to continue doing. [146] His followers are reluctant to challenge him.

The dysfunctional family patterns that we learned early in life are carried unconsciously into any community we join. Christina Grof writes, "We take with us vulnerability, shame and guilt, lack of personal boundaries, dependency, codependency, and a need to control or be controlled. We carry our projections, our need for power, our tendency to idealize, or our unwillingness to doubt. In addition, a spiritual community or therapeutic setting seems to offer a sanctuary from our own pain, our past, and our addictive culture". [147]

The combinations of ethical vulnerabilities in this situation often include most, if not all, of the issues of the seven centers. Christina Grof counsels, "Any good spiritual teacher will serve only as a guide who always points us toward ourselves, consistently throwing us back on our own resources."[148] In contrast, she points out, "Manipulative teachers and therapists . . . often abuse people who place their trust in them, exploiting them financially, sexually, emotionally, and spiritually. In addition they help to create religious or therapeutic dependence."[149]

Organizational support of personal growth for practitioners

A professional organization can set the tone of valuing direct experience in nonordinary states for its practitioners. It can set aside a significant portion of training time or hours qualifying for licensure or certification for required, direct nonordinary state experience. The community can also provide continuing education and training regarding ethical issues that arise in work with clients who are experiencing profound or intense times in therapy. In this way the organization expands its understanding of ethics not just as a list of "don'ts," but as a long list of self-exploratory "do's."

Uniting to defend the ethics and efficacy of a particular system

Many systems which use techniques to induce powerful and profound states of consciousness are still on the fringe of mainstream psychology and religion. It can be considered legally unethical to practice an innovative technique with a client unless that technique has some proven value. Practitioners of that technique may not be able to demonstrate its therapeutic value by scientific research nor do they have the rationale that it has been accepted by a critical mass of traditionally certified professionals.

One of the purposes which communities and formal organizations serve is to demonstrate that a particular system is effective for healing or spiritual exploration and growth. The organization has numbers of members (practitioners and clients) who agree that there is therapeutic value in the method. The organization can proceed to share information among its members and begin to consider an ethical code of conduct. A community that has thought out the conditions for ethical practice of its method and has had them adopted by its membership is in a better position to defend its technique if its practice should be questioned.

Humane response to ethics problems

The organization can support truth-telling by taking a humane position toward those who learn ethical behavior by making mistakes. If a therapist has stumbled into an ethical pitfall and wishes to tell the truth about it and go on with his practice, is there any incentive to do so?

What incentive could there be for an individual to break the taboo preventing openness about ethical misconduct and restart her practice with a cleaned slate? Organizations could encourage their professionals to form peer supervision groups by providing some inducement to those who do so.

How could organizations put their emphasis on constructive learning rather than on punishment? Organizations can review their disciplinary committee's actions to see if their response to an unethical action serves the community, the clients, and the individual therapist involved. They can review their codes to see if it is possible to make their ethical guidelines less complex. The more simple and flexible the guidelines are, the more humane the ethics committee can be in fitting their response to the situation.

Working to change codes as necessary

Not all ethical actions are professionally "ethical" or even legal. A suit-happy society can move easily in an unethical direction. Caregivers can actually become afraid to take risks, to confront or challenge clients, or take actions they know in their hearts to be the most ethical choices. Ethics committees promoting an external locus of control wield voluminous codes and sub-codes. The codes and procedures for disciplinary actions can engender fear of misunderstanding and reprisal. Ethics committees attempting to develop an internal locus of control can emphasize training, discussion, and encourage truth-telling. They can consult experts on countertransference, especially those with experience working with clients in nonordinary states, to insure that they have addressed the subtleties of each case. They can craft a simple, humane code of ethics, which is flexible enough to administer appropriately.

Organizational Actions For Expanding Ethical Awareness

■ Support truth-telling

■ Encourage members to form peer supervision groups

■ Require experiential training in nonordinary states as part of hours qualifying for certification or licensure

■ Encourage training in countertransference issues

■ Review ethics codes to see if they are simple and flexible

■ Review ethics codes to see if they incorporate statements relevant to working with clients in nonordinary states

■ Allow ethics committees to respond as individually appropriate to cases of ethical misconduct

■ Incorporate expert opinion into decisions regarding cases of ethical misconduct

15

Creating Ethical Guidelines

Expanding ethical consciousness through written codes

When something is written down in this culture, it gains credibility and begins to shape the way people think and act. It is an art to write something that sets a general tone and provides a structure or standard but at the same time, allows for interpretation as appropriate in individual cases and for evolution over time.

Language that reflects the understanding gained from work with intense states of consciousness might enhance some ethical codes. Ethical guidelines that address such ethical issues might begin to shape ethics education and efforts aimed toward preventing ethical misconduct.

I have looked at a number of codes of therapeutic organizations. The sample I used contained codes from the large traditional associations and from medium to small organizations whose members practice a particular technique which induces nonordinary states of consciousness in clients. One code in the sample was a statement from a religion for its spiritual teachers. I have chosen representative statements from this sample that apply to the issues I have described in each of the seven centers and to each of the keys to professional ethical behavior.

I am not advocating the use of any of these wordings. I offer these excerpts only to generate organizational self-reflection for those who want to re-examine their existing code or draft one that meets the needs of their particular members. This section is for those who want some direction in creating or adding to their own ethical codes. It offers examples of specific language which pertains to the theory and practice of therapeutic techniques which may induce nonordinary states.

Preambles to ethical codes

Somewhere in an ethical code, usually at the beginning, an organization defines the bigger picture relative to the organization's particular work. The code describes the greater effect this practicing community hopes to have by acting ethically and effectively in its own sphere. Here are two examples:

> *Our aim is to increase the client's access to the complex relations between energetic, emotions, and structural phenomena in his or her body; to evoke his or her inherent ability to live in harmony with physical reality; and to establish a structure which will allow him or her to creatively employ physical energies for the evolution of all.*[150]

> *Members recognize their intrinsic involvement in the total community on planet Earth.*[151]

Ethical codes and money

The issues of the first center are money, change, security, and sufficiency. Most ethical codes have written sections on honest practice. Here is one that simply links honesty and consciousness to respect for all resources.

> *Beyond our fundamental agreement to respect the property of others, we agreed to bring consciousness to the use of all of the earth's resources, to be honest in our dealings with money.*[152]

In the following code written by several Emotional Release Counsellors Associations in Australia, counselors are to make clear agreements with their clients. These include agreements that the clients will not damage persons or property during a session, will not engage in sexual behavior with others in a group session, will complete sessions and workshops unless their contract is re-negotiated with their counselor, and will respect the confidentiality of other participants in group work. The code includes a section on providing informed consent, particularly focusing on work with clients in non-ordinary states of consciousness:

> *A counsellor gives the client a description of, a rationale for, and possible outcomes of participation in an ERC session. The counsellor gives the client information on integration and follow-up, and options for on-going support. The counsellor clearly presents the contraindications for participation in ERC work generally and Transpersonal Breathwork in particular, as well as requiring information on client's medical condition, so that the counsellor and the client together decide whether participation is appropriate.*[153]

The same code also includes the following example, which is found in some form in almost every ethics code:

> *A counsellor shall maintain clear and honest business practices, including agreements regarding appointment and workshop times and fees.*[154]

Ethical codes and sex

Statistically, sex is the area of greatest ethical concern. Most ethical codes stipulate what is unethical sexual behavior with clients. Because of the tendency for impulsive response when one is sexually attracted to a client, most professional codes of ethics are very clear about prohibiting sexual contact with clients. The American Group Psychotherapy Association, Inc., says: *sexual intimacy with patients/clients is unethical.*[155] The American Association for Marriage and Family Therapy says: *Sexual intimacy with clients is prohibited.*[156] The American Psychiatric Association says: *Sexual activity with a current or former patient is unethical.*

Clarity is even more important in the confusing situation where physical desire and spiritual longing intersect and where the tendency to rationalize sexual behavior is most strong. These are two resolute statements that make such rationalization difficult:

> *The level of trust engendered by ERC makes it important to avoid any sexual harm or exploitation.*[157]

> *We do not invite, project, respond to, or allow any sexual contact with our clients or apprentices.*[158]

The Rolf Institute, which practices a form of bodywork, writes in its *Code of Ethics:*

> *We protect the welfare of any person who may <u>seek our services</u>. [Emphasis in original.] We do not use our professional position or relationship for purposes inconsistent with our values. We do not attempt to transfer the authority of the teaching relationship . . . to other associations with our clients, realizing that <u>sexual relations</u> or the imposition of opinions, prejudices, or personal preferences of any kind is detrimental to the welfare of our clients. We take care to insure an appropriate setting in our practice . . . to protect our clients and ourselves from actual or imputed harm and the profession from censure.*[159]

The Insight Meditation Teachers of Buddhist meditation have done an admirable job of highlighting the reasons for their agreements among themselves about refraining from sexual conduct with students. They also suggest guidelines for sensitively managing the occasional genuine relationship that develops between a teacher and an ex-student. Following the precept of refraining from causing harm through sexual behavior, the teachers agree that:

a) *A sexual relationship is never appropriate between teachers and students.*

b) *During retreats or formal teaching, any intimation of future student-teacher romantic or sexual relationship is inappropriate.*

c) *If a genuine and committed relationship interest develops over time between an unmarried teacher and a former student, the student must clearly be under the guidance of another teacher. Such a relationship must be approached with restraint and sensitivity—in no case should it occur immediately after retreat. A minimum time period of three months or longer from the last formal teaching between them, and a clear understanding from both parties that the student-teacher relationship has ended must be coupled with a conscious commitment to enter into a relationship that brings no harm to either party.* [160]

Ethical codes and power

Ethical codes usually acknowledge the power of a caregiver to exploit clients. Some of them talk about the appropriate use of power as well. It seems particularly important also to acknowledge the positive capability of power to empower.

*As Rolfers, our goal is to introduce a structure and
provide the information that will enable the [client] to
use his or her physical self to its fullest capacity.*[161]

*JSDF members respect the client's physical /emotional
state, and do not abuse clients through actions, words,
or silence, nor take advantage of the therapeutic relationship . . . . [They] honor the client's requests as much
as possible within personal, professional and ethical
limits.*[162]

*As Rolfers, we consider that the client is the best and
final authority about his or her own welfare. We seek
at all times to further that understanding; at no time
do we endeavor to assume that function ourselves.*[163]

*A feminist therapist acknowledges the inherent power
differentials between client and therapist, and models
effective use of personal power. In using the power
differential to the benefit of the client, she does not
take control or power which rightfully belongs to her
client.*[164]

Ethical codes and love

Perhaps unsurprisingly, the word *love* does not appear in
ethical codes I have read. *Compassion* and *caring* do appear in
most codes. This is the paragraph I found that speaks most directly
to the issues of the fourth center:

■   *We recognize that competition, mistrust, or the
spreading of rumors destroys the spirit of kindness
and union which is the heart of any human association.*[165]

Ethical codes and truth

Truth-telling is mentioned as *honesty* in many codes. Here are
two examples of codes which go a bit farther than most in emphasizing honesty:

■ *We agreed to speak that which is true and useful, to refrain from gossip in our community, to cultivate conscious and clear communication, and to cultivate the quality of loving-kindness and honesty as the basis of our speech.*[166]

■ *JSDF members maintain clear and honest communications with their clients.*[167]

Ethical codes and insight

This example addresses some of the ethical issues discussed in the chapter on the sixth center.

■ *Nonordinary states of Holotropic Breathwork mobilize intrinsic healing forces in the psyche and the body. As this process is unfolding, this inner healer manifests therapeutic wisdom which transcends the knowledge that can be derived from the cognitive understanding of an individual practitioner or from any specific school of psychotherapy or body work.*[168]

Ethical codes and oneness

I could not find any sections in ethical codes which address the issues of the seventh center directly. One code, however, in respecting spiritual autonomy, specifically allows the client freedom to have extraordinary, anomalous, or spiritually diverse experiences. This freedom of spiritual expression is important to stress when the client encounters experiences which are difficult for the caregiver to affirm. (See *Chapter 3*.)

■ *We respect the emotional, physical, mental, and spiritual autonomy of our clients.*[169]

Ethical codes and authentic caring

In my mind caring is the most important attribute of an ethical therapist or caregiver. I found that most ethical codes seemed to assume caring but not mention it very directly. Here are two examples that do talk about caring:

> ◢ *To establish and maintain trust in the client relationship, they are encouraged to ask caring questions about the client's well-being, and to establish clear boundaries and an atmosphere of safety.*[170]

> ■ *As Rolfers, we respect the human dignity of each individual with whom we are associated in our profession. We are guided at all times by the welfare of the clients who have entrusted themselves to our care.*[171]

The code I found which was clear and most concise on caring was from the code of the American Psychiatric Association.

> ■ *A physician shall be dedicated to providing competent medical service with compassion and respect for human dignity.*[172]

Ethical codes and willingness to examine our own motivations

The value of being willing to examine one's own motivations, crucial though it is to a professional therapist/client relationship (or any relationship,) is rarely included as such in professional codes. Competence is most often equated with adequate training. It may be inferred that adequate training includes self-reflection, but perhaps that should not be left to inference. What is explicitly written down often becomes what is emphasized.

My own graduate school preparation (and, I suspect, that of many others) offered a great deal of "training" and memorization. It focused on diagnosis of the client and learning interventions but provided little encouragement for observing one's own countertransference in one's professional practice and for beginning a life-long practice of self-reflection and self-disclosure to one's supervisors and peers. The following example sets the tone for self-examination by professionals:

■
As individuals or as individuals working in organizations, we subscribe to the value of self-examination in order to promote personal growth in ethics.[173]

Ethical codes and willingness to ask for help

Communities can probably avoid a conflict between those in authority handing down ethical codes and "mere members" who feel they have been forced to abide by them. One way to avoid this situation is to have members participate in drawing up *agreements* and then committing to them formally at the beginning of training and at licensure, ordination, or certification. The following agreement is comprehensive, brief, and simple. It appears on the application for membership and requires a signature. A representative of The American Association of Professional Hypnotherapists stated that this short ethical agreement has served them well for several years.[174]

I agree to utilize hypnosis only within the areas of my expertise and in accordance with applicable law, to maintain the highest ethical and professional standards, and to keep the interests and welfare of those who seek my help above all other considerations.[175]

The following agreement pledges practitioners to monitor their own neutrality with regard to clients and their own fitness for service.

We will respect the rights, dignity, and individuality of each patient, strongly separating our professional practice of healing from any personal, religious, racial, or sexual considerations, referring out to another practitioner immediately should this become apparent, and by avoiding the treatment of patients if impaired by physical or mental inadequacy or by chemical dependency.[176]

This following section of an ethical code covers the loopholes in encouraging members to ask for help when in doubt. It also encourages community consultation and feedback:

> *When a psychologist is uncertain whether a particular situation or course of action would violate this Ethics Code, the psychologist ordinarily consults with other psychologists knowledgeable about ethical issues, with state or national ethics committees, or with other appropriate authorities in order to choose a proper response.*[177]

Skilled analysis of therapeutic and counter-therapeutic interventions in cases of ethical misconduct

Many ethical codes outline their procedures for dealing with misconduct. It is not the purpose of this book to talk about investigation of ethical complaints or disciplinary procedure. However, I want to highlight one suggestion by Lawrence Hedges that might be useful in reviewing misconduct cases that involve nonordinary states of consciousness.

Hedges, in writing about preventing and dealing with exploitative dual relationships, makes a suggestion that is relevant also to the multiple functions a therapist or caregiver assumes when working with a client in nonordinary states. He points out that there are no rigorous experiential training qualifications for those who sit on such boards. He suggests that expert consultants be appointed to advise the regular ethics committee or governing board. He defines experts with advanced knowledge of the subtleties of transference and countertransference as therapists having approximately fifteen years of advanced training, supervision, practice, and personal transference analysis.[178] In cases when a client has been inducted into a nonordinary state of consciousness by her therapist, I would add more to Hedges definition of *expert*. In my opinion, an expert in these cases would also have had considerable experience with nonordinary states of consciousness in general and the method under indictment in particular.

Hedges points out that boards and committees who make decisions about practitioners' licenses are often in a position of conflict of interest because of political pressure, consumer interests, or fear of negative publicity. Seeking advice from a panel of impartial experts would serve the best interests of the client who has brought the complaint, as well as the best interests of the board, the organization, and the professional whose reputation has been indicted.

Creating our own inner "ethical codes"

Written ethical codes describe the values of an organization of practitioners. Organizations publish ethical guidelines as a reminder to themselves and a message to others about the integrity of the organization.

Establishing an ethical code is an exercise in self-reflection and clarification of values for those who write, review, and approve such documents. The process of establishing internal rather than external locus of control with regard to ethics must continue after codes are published. Each person who begins considering her ethical values starts the process anew within herself by questioning, observing, discussing, and experimenting.

Ethical codes cannot ensure ethical action, but they can help prevent ethical misconduct if used as outlines for discussion in continuing education and training. If classes and peer supervision groups encourage truly open discussion about ethical issues, practitioners and students will feel permission to explore the elements of a professional healing relationship and uncover their own vulnerabilities and personal motivations.

Each of us as caregivers must formulate his or her own sense of what is right relationship to a client. Only our courageous soul-searching can bring consciousness to the fears, desires, and spiritual longings hidden in each of our shadows.

Glossary

Archetype—A representation of some principle or quality in symbolic form.

Basic Perinatal Matrix (BPM)—Stanislav Grof described four matrices, which are stages in the birth process: BPM I, II, III, and IV. (See below.)

BPM I—The stage in the birth process before labor begins. Also, the stage in any major life process in which there is a sense of being cared for, of ripening and fulfillment, and perhaps, of imminent change.

BPM II—The stage in the birth process after labor begins, but before the cervix is dilated. The fetus is stuck. This is also the stage of any major life change or process, especially at the beginning of a transition, in which there are feelings of being overwhelmed, and of helplessness, hopelessness, timelessness, depression, and victimization.

BPM III—The stage in the birth process after the cervix is dilated and the fetus is moving down the birth canal. Also, the stage of any major life change or process in which there is struggle, conflict, energy or aggression, movement, and empowerment.

BPM IV—Birth, transition from life as a fetus to life as a newborn baby. Also, the stage of the birth process (or any major life change or process) in which there is surrender, breakthrough, death/rebirth, completion, and resolution.

Breather—This is the term for the breathwork participant who is lying down, breathing, and entering a nonordinary state of consciousness. In Holotropic Breathwork™, the breather alternately plays the role of the sitter for her partner.

Breathwork—Experiential work, using accelerated and deepened breathing that precipitates a nonordinary state of consciousness. Breathwork is done both individually with a therapist or facilitator and in groups.

COEX system—Stanislav Grof's term for a collection of experiences that are linked to each other through a particular event, body symptom, sensation, or emotion.

Cognitive dissonance—An internal struggle in which one belief or set of beliefs challenges the validity of another belief or set of beliefs.

Cosmic consciousness—A state beyond words in which one identifies with all of creation.

Countertransference—The caregiver reacts unconsciously to the client's feelings, thoughts, expectations, and beliefs and may project his own feelings, thoughts, expectations, patterns of behavior, and beliefs onto the client.

Defense mechanism—Coping styles that are employed automatically and most often unconsciously to protect the individual from becoming aware of internal or external dangers or anxieties.

Dissociation—Disconnection internally between thoughts and feelings or intuitions or sensations or between one part of the psyche's thoughts, feelings, intuitions, and sensations and another part of the psyche's thoughts, feelings, intuitions and sensations.

Dual (or multiple) relationship—A relationship between a professional and a client in which the professional interacts with the client in a social, familial, business, political, religious, or other context which is beyond her professional role.

Focused energy release work—A system of techniques used to help Holotropic Breathwork participants amplify, experience fully, and release physical symptoms that arise during breathwork.

Grof Maps of Consciousness—Four categories of experiences that occur in nonordinary states of consciousness: sensory, biographical, perinatal, and transpersonal.

Higher Power—Spirit or God as one understands Spirit or God. A concept greater than the individual self.

Holotropic—Christina and Stanislav Grof coined this term from Greek root words which mean *moving toward wholeness.*

Holotropic Breathwork™—The term trademarked by the Grofs to describe the particular style of breathwork done by those certified by the Grof Transpersonal Training. Holotropic Breathwork uses accelerated breathing, art, music, and focused energy release work.

Informed consent—The agreement by a client to undergo a treatment or participate in a technique after being thoroughly apprised of the method and the possible results of doing so.

Kundalini—A Sanskrit word describing the evolutionary life force. In human beings it is said to lie dormant at the base of the spine until awakened. When awakened it moves through the physical, mental, and spiritual aspects of one's being to purify and make the psyche more conscious. It is also the name of the Hindu Goddess, Kundalini Shakti, who represents manifest energy and matter.

Lucid dreaming—Consciousness of a dream while dreaming; having a degree of control of the content or direction of the dream while asleep.

Multiplicity—A high degree of dissociation usually created unconsciously in order to cope with severe trauma. Parts of the personality and memory are separated from other parts. This phenomenon has been called Multiple Personality Disorder, and is currently termed *Dissociative Identity Disorder* in the DSM IV.

Near death experience (NDE)—An experience of beginning the dying process but then returning to life characterized by certain patterns of images and experiences and by significant changes in perspective.

Nonordinary state of consciousness—A normal and expanded consciousness that promotes healing, reconnection with self, others, and nature, and psychospiritual development and insight.

Ordinary state of consciousness—A normal and usual state of consciousness useful in functional daily life.

Peak experiences—Experiences in which one ecstatically transcends the usual limited perspective of self and life.

Perinatal—A term describing the experiences immediately prior to, during, and immediately after birth.

Pre-cognition—Knowledge of an event before it happens.

Process—In the psychological and spiritual sense, it is used loosely to describe the events, the emotions, the insights, as well as the method, the movement, and the integration of developing consciousness.

Psychic flooding—A opening of the mind to intuitive images and concepts so that one feels no ability to refuse the incoming information.

Psychospiritual—A term designed to describe the interrelationship of the mind, emotions, and spirit in one's process or experiences.

Relive—Experience again with more awareness of sensation, emotion, and cognition than was experienced when it first occurred (during birth, this biographical life, or what seems to be a past life).

Rolfing—A system of deep muscle massage which seeks to realign or structurally integrate the body.

Shamanic—Having to do with shamans (tribal wise persons or healers) who use various natural methods to enter nonordinary states in order to seek healing or wisdom for themselves and their communities.

Sitter—The person who sits beside the person who is experiencing a nonordinary state of consciousness and provides attention and response to her requests according to the contract between the two. In Holotropic Breathwork, the sitter alternately plays the role of breather with her partner as sitter.

Soul retrieval—The technique whereby a competent shaman journeys in nonordinary reality to find a lost or dissociated part of the client and then through nonordinary means helps the client reclaim that part.

Spiritual emergence—The psychospiritual development of self, involving major changes in beliefs, emotions, insight, and relationship to body, others, world, and God.

Spiritual emergency—Rapid or dramatic psychospiritual development in which a person becomes partially or fully dysfunctional for a period of time.

Spiritual Emergence Network—An information and referral service which provides mental health options to those in psychospiritual crisis.

Spontaneous nonordinary state—A state which is normal, but not usual, and which was not induced intentionally. Spontaneous nonordinary states can occur during childbirth, orgasm, deep grief, accidents, illness, or spiritual emergency.

Tantra—A system of Eastern spiritual practices that seekers practice in order to move beyond duality to unity. Commonly referred to as the specific sexual practices which use the sexual energy and life force to achieve spiritual ecstasy and enlightenment.

Trance—A deep state in which the attention is narrowed and focused.

Transference—The client reacts unconsciously to the caregiver's feelings, thoughts, expectations, patterns of behavior, and beliefs and may project his own feelings, thoughts, expectations, and beliefs onto the caregiver.

Transpersonal—Describes those phenomena that take place outside the boundaries of our personal identity or self or beyond time and space.

Trauma reenactment—Reliving the same pattern of trauma experienced earlier in life. The re-enactment is characterized by the same pattern of behaviors, thoughts, emotions, body sensations, and perceptions as in the first experience of trauma. Trauma re-enactment can be therapeutic (intentional abreaction with awareness) or counter-therapeutic (unconscious replication of victimization in daily life.)

Trauma of commission—Something that happened in the past with such intensity that it could not be fully experienced and assimilated at the time it occurred, resulting in lingering effects in the present.

Trauma of omission—Something that did not happen at the time that it was needed so that the lack of it in the past (*e.g.,* nurturance, warmth, food, protection) continues to affect the present experience.

Twelve Steps—A list of twelve principles and action steps, written by the founders of Alcoholics Anonymous, that map a path to recovery from addiction.

UFO abduction—A reported experience of encounter with aliens from outer space and of being used as a research subject by these beings, usually accompanied by symptoms of post-traumatic stress and sometimes accompanied by synchronistic physical signs.

Unitive experience—An experience in which one feels one with all and a part of everything in creation.

$\mathcal{E}$nd Notes

[1] Manning, R.C. (1992). *Speaking from the heart: A feminist perspective on ethics.* Lanham, MD: Rowman & Littlefield Publishers, Inc. xiv.

[2] Havel, V. (1994). Unpublished speech given at Stanford University. September 29, 1994.

[3] *Ibid.*

[4] Remen, R. N. (Autumn, 1988). On defining spirit. *Noetic Sciences Review.* 63.

[5] *Ibid.*

[6] Keith-Spiegel, P. & Koocher, G. B. (1985). *Ethics in psychology: Professional standards and cases.* New York: Random House. 6.

[7] Gilligan, C. (1982). *In a different voice: Psychological theory and women's development.* Cambridge, MA: Harvard University Press. 20-63.

[8] Manning, R. (1992). *Speaking from the heart: A feminist perspective on ethics.* Lanham, MD: Rowman & Littlefield Publishers, Inc. xiv.

[9] Wylie, M.S. (Mar/Apr, 1989). The ethical therapist: Looking for the fence posts. *The Family Therapy Networker.* Washington, D.C. 24.

[10] Schweitzer, A. (1966). *Reverence for life.* New York: Harper & Row Publishers. 116.

[11] Bartlett, J. (1968). [14th Ed.] *Familiar quotations.* Boston: Little, Brown and Company. 939.

[12] *The Bible.* Luke 6:31.

[13] Taylor, K. (1994). *The breathwork experience: Exploration and healing in nonordinary states of consciousness.* Santa Cruz, CA: Hanford Mead Publishers. 13-14.

[14] *Ibid.*

[15] *Ibid.*

[16] Ludwig, A. M. (1966). In Tart, C. [Ed.] (1969) (1972). *Altered states of consciousness.* Garden City, New York: Anchor Books. 11.

[17] Wolinsky, S. (1991). *Trances people live: Healing approaches to quantum psychology.* Falls Village, CT: The Bramble Company.

[18] Grof, C. & Grof, S. (1990). *The stormy search for the self: A guide to personal growth through transformational crisis.* Los Angeles: Jeremy P. Tarcher, Inc. 73-99.

Grof, S. (1985). *Beyond the brain.* Albany, NY: State University of New York Press. 38-41.

Grof, C. (1993). *The thirst for wholeness: Attachment, addiction and the spiritual path.* New York: HarperCollins. 12, 15-16.

[19] Browne, I. (Spring 1990). Psychological trauma, or unexperienced experience. *ReVision* 12, 21-33.

[20] Grof, S. (1985). *Beyond the brain.* Albany, NY: State University of New York Press. 251-52.

Taylor, K. (1994). *The breathwork experience: Exploration and healing in nonordinary states of consciousness.* Santa Cruz, CA: Hanford Mead Publishers. 64.

[21] Ingerman, S. (1991). *Soul retrieval: Mending the fragmented self.* San Francisco: HarperCollins.

[22] Kripalvanand, S. (1975). *The stages of kundalini yoga.* Sumneytown, Pennsylvania: Kripalu Yoga Ashram.

Krishna, G. (1971). *Kundalini: The evolutionary energy in man.* Berkeley, CA: Shambhala.

Muktananda, S. (1974). *Play of consciousness.* Oakland, CA: S.Y.D.A. Foundation.

Narayanananda, S. (1979). *The primal power in man or the kundalini shakti.* Gylling, Denmark: N.U. Yoga Trust & Ashram.

Sannella, L. (1976). *Kundalini: Psychosis or transcendence?* San Francisco: H.S. Dakin Company.

[23] Ring, K. (1984). *Heading toward omega: In search of the meaning of the near-death experience.* New York: William Morrow and Company, Inc. 41-44.

Moody, R.A. (1976). *Life after life.* Harrisburg, PA: Stackpole Books. 31-43.

[24] Ring, K. (1980). *Life at death: A scientific investigation of the near-death experience.* New York: Coward, McCann & Geoghegan.

Ring, K. (1984). *Heading toward omega: In search of the meaning of the near-death experience.* New York: William Morrow and Company, Inc.

Moody, R.A. (1976). *Life after life.* Harrisburg, PA: Stackpole Books.

Reader, L. (Summer, 1994). The internal mystery plays: The role and physiology of the visual system in contemplative practices. *ReVision.* 3-13.

[25] Grof, C. & Grof, S. (1990). *The stormy search for the self: A guide to personal growth through transformational crisis.* Los Angeles: Jeremy P. Tarcher, Inc. 73-99.

[26] Mack, J. (1994). *Abductions.* New York: Charles Scribner's Sons. 32.

[27] *Ibid.* 15-16.

[28] Ross, C. (1989). *Multiple personality disorder.* New York: John Wiley & Sons. 183-85.

[29] Smith, M. (1993). *Ritual abuse.* San Francisco: HarperCollins.

Smith, M. (1993). *It's love and unity I want.* Woodland, CA: Reaching Out.

[30] Taylor, K. (1994). *The breathwork experience:* Santa Cruz, CA: Hanford Mead Publishers. 49-88.

[31] Hart, M. (1990). *Drumming on the edge of magic.* New York: HarperCollins Publishers. 176-77.

[32] Institute for Music, Health, & Education. PO Box 4179, Boulder, CO 80306-4179. (303) 443-0053.

[33] Who and what is Network Chiropractic? (1993). *Network chiropractic alignment for growth.* Innate Intelligence, Inc. 1(4) 1.

[34] Wolinsky, S. (1991). *Trances people live: Healing approaches to quantum psychology.* Falls Village, CT: The Bramble Company. 9.

[35] Shapiro, F. (1989a). Efficacy of the eye movement desensitization procedure in the treatment of traumatic memories. *Journal of Traumatic Stress.* 2, 199-223.

[36] Kornfield, J. (1993). *A path with heart: A guide through the perils and promises of spiritual life.* New York: Bantam. 122-26.

[37] Shor, R.E. (1959). In Tart, C. [Ed.] (1969) (1972). *Altered states of consciousness.* Garden City, New York: Anchor Books. 247.

[38] *Ibid.* 255.

[39] The Foundation for Shamanic Studies, PO Box 1709, Mill Valley, CA 94942.

[40] Achterberg, J. (1985). *Imagery in healing.* Boston: New Science Library. 37-45.

Ott, J. (1993). *Pharmacotheon.* Kennewick, WA: Natural Products.

[41] Savage, C., Savage, E., Fadiman, J., & Harman, W. (1964). *LSD: Therapeutic effects of the psychedelic experience.* Psychol. Rep., 14. 111-20.

[42] Grof, S. (1975). *Realms of the human unconscious: Observations from LSD research.* New York: The Viking Press.

MacLean, J., MacDonald, D., Byrne, U., and Hubbard, A. (1961). The use of LSD-25 in the treatment of alcoholism and other psychiatric problems. *Quarterly Journal on Studies of Alcoholism.* 22. 34-35.

Sherwood, J., Stolaroff, M., and Harman, W. (1962). The psychedelic experience: A new concept in psychotherapy. *Journal of Neuropsychiatry.* 4. 69-80.

[43] Grof, S. (1977). *The human encounter with death.* London: Souvenir Press.

[44] Doblin, R. (1995). Personal conversation.

[45] Doblin, R. (1992). Historic FDA and NIDA meetings. Multi-

disciplinary Association for Psychedelic Studies, Inc. *MAPS Newsletter*. III (3) 2-6.

[46] Mindell, A. (1993). *The shaman's body*. San Francisco: HarperSanFrancisco.

[47] *Ibid.* 169.

[48] Kornfield, J. (1993). *The path with heart: A guide through the perils and promises of spiritual life*. New York: Bantam. 133.

[49] Grof, S. (1977). *The human encounter with death*. London: Souvenir Press.

[50] Grof, S. (1985). *Beyond the brain*. Albany, NY: State University of New York Press. 38-41.

[51] Spence, D. P. (1982). *Narrative truth and historical truth: Meaning and interpretation in psychoanalysis*. New York: W.W. Norton & Co., Inc. 175.

[52] *Ibid.* 270.

[53] Meacham, A. (April, 1993). Presumed guilty. *Changes*. 78.

[54] Herman, J. (1992). *Trauma and recovery*. New York: Basic Books. 179.

[55] The Australian Psychological Society Limited (October, 1994). Guidelines relating to the reporting of recovered memories. In *FMS Foundation Newsletter*. (January, 1995). 7.

[56] American Psychiatric Association. (1994). Statement on memories of sexual abuse. Washington: D.C. 2, 5.

[57] Grof, S. & Ross, C. (Speakers) (Audiotape) (June, 1993). *Advanced Holotropic Breathwork training in multiple personality disorder*. Boulder, CO: Sounds True Recordings.

[58] Sparks, C. (1993). COEX systems and biographical trauma: Working multi-dimensionally in Holotropic Breathwork. *The Inner Door*. Santa Cruz, CA: Association for Holotropic Breathwork International. 5 (1) 1,4.

[59] Wylie, M.S. (Mar/Apr, 1989). The ethical therapist: looking for fenceposts. *The Family Therapy Networker*. Washington, D.C. 26.

[60] Grof, S. (1985). *Beyond the brain*. Albany, NY: State University of New York Press. 38-41.

[61] Eliade, M. (1964). *Shamanism: Archaic techniques of ecstasy*. Princeton, NJ: Princeton University Press.

[62] *Ibid.*

[63] Taylor, K. (1994). *The breathwork experience: Exploration and healing in nonordinary states of consciousness*. Santa Cruz, CA: Hanford Mead Publishers. 33.

[64] Grof, S. (1980). *LSD Psychotherapy*. Pomona, CA: Hunter House, Inc. Publishers. 257-59.

[65] *Diagnostic and statistical manual of mental disorders*. Fourth edition. Washington, D.C. American Psychiatric Association. 685.

[66] Grof, S. (1980). *LSD psychotherapy.* Pomona, CA: Hunter House, Inc. Publishers. 101.

[67] Brown, D. P. & Fromm, E. (1986). *Hypnotherapy and hypnoanalysis.* Hillsdale, NJ: Lawrence Erlbaum Associates, Publishers. 143.

[68] Salter, S. & Ness, C. (1993). *San Francisco Examiner.* April 9, 1993. A-18.

[69] Grof, S. & Grof, C. (1990). Principles of Holotropic Breathwork. In Taylor, K. (1991). *The Holotropic Breathwork workshop: A manual for trained facilitators.* 79.

[70] Pope, K. S. & Vasquez, M. J. T. (1991). *Ethics in psychotherapy.* San Francisco: Jossey Bass, Inc. 75.

[71] Steele, K. (1993). (Speaker*). Issues in the treatment of multiple personality disorder.* (Audiotape). Longmont, CO: Genesis II Seminars and Products.

[72] Scheller, M. D. (Autumn/Winter, 1992-93). To touch or not to touch: Legal, ethical, and clinical issues concerning the incorporation of nonsexual touch into verbal psychotherapy. *Somatics.* 42-45.

[73] Grof, S. (1988). *The adventure of self-discovery.* Albany, NY: State University of New York Press. 198-99.

[74] Herman, J. (1992). *Trauma and recovery.* New York: Basic Books. 187.

[75] Grof, S. (1980). *LSD Psychotherapy.* Pomona, CA: Hunter House, Inc. Publishers. 101.

Leary, T., Metzner, R., and Alpert, R. (1964). *The psychedelic experience.* Secaucus, NJ: The Citadel Press. 111.

[76] Brown, D. P. & Fromm, E. (1986). *Hypnotherapy and hypnoanalysis.* Hillsdale, NJ: Lawrence Erlbaum Associates, Publishers.

[77] Herman, J. (1992). *Trauma and recovery.* New York: Basic Books. 143-47.

Calof, D. (1993). (Speaker) *Adult children of incest and child abuse.* (Audiotape) Longmont, CO: Genesis II Seminars and Projects.

[78] Rutter, P. (1989). *Sex in the forbidden zone.* Los Angeles: Jeremy P. Tarcher. 145.

[79] *Ibid.* 55.

[80] Kornfield, J. (1993). *Teachings of the Buddha.* Boston: Shambhala Publications, Inc. 42.

[81] Judith, A. (1987). *Wheels of life.* St. Paul, MN: Lewellyn Publications. 60, 112, 166, 210, 258, 314, 391-3.

[82] *The Bible.* Luke 6:31.

[83] *The Bible.* Matthew 7:3.

[84] Grof, C. (1993). *The thirst for wholeness: Attachment, addiction and the spiritual path.* New York: HarperCollins. 12, 15-16.

[85] Grof, S. (1980). *LSD Psychotherapy.* Pomona, CA: Hunter House, Inc. Publishers. 107.

[86] Bragdon, E. (1990*). The call of spiritual emergency.* San Francisco, CA: Harper & Row, Publishers.

Bragdon, E. (1988). *A sourcebook for helping people in spiritual emergency.* Los Altos, CA: Lightening Up Press.

Grof, S. & Grof, C. (Eds.). (1989). *Spiritual emergency: When personal transformation becomes a crisis.* Los Angeles: Jeremy Tarcher.

Grof, C. & Grof, S. (1990). *The stormy search for the self: A guide to personal growth through transformational crisis.* Los Angeles: Jeremy P. Tarcher.

Muktananda, S. (1974). *Play of consciousness.* Oakland, CA: S.Y.D.A. Foundation.

[87] Guggenbühl-Craig, A. (1971, 1982). *Power in the Helping Professions.* Dallas, TX: Spring Publications, Inc. 63

[88] Grof, S. (1985). *Beyond the brain.* Albany, NY: State University of New York Press. 202-203.

[89] Grof, S. (February, 1993). Training discussion at Grof Transpersonal Training, St. Helena, CA.

[90] Pope, K. S. & Bouhoutsos, J. C. (1986). *Sexual intimacy between therapists and patients.* New York: Praeger. 10.

[91] Scheller, M.D. (Autumn/Winter 1992-93). To touch or not to touch: Legal, ethical, and clinical issues concerning the incorporation of nonsexual touch into verbal psychotherapy. *Somatics.* 42-43.

[92] *Ibid.* 44.

[93] Pope, K. S. (August, 1994). Sexual involvement between therapists and patients. *The Harvard Mental Health Letter.* 5.

[94] Peay, P. S. (Jul/Aug, 1994). What do women want. *Common Boundary.* 12 (4) 22-34.

[95] Berne, E. (1954). *Games people play.* New York: Grove Press. 151-154.

[96] Ziegler, K. *Personal communication.*

[97] Sparks, T., Sparks, C., Gitkind, H., and Jefferys, B. (1989). Unpublished paper. *Doing, not doing: A facilitator's guide to holotropic focused body work.* 17.

[98] Achterberg, J. (1985). *Imagery in healing.* Boston: New Science Library. 26-27.

[99] *The Bible.* Matthew 4:1-10.

[100] Guggenbühl-Craig, A. (1971, 1982) *Power in the helping professions.* Dallas, TX: Spring Publications, Inc. 38-39.

[101] Karpman, S. B. (1968). Fairy tales and script drama analysis. *Transactional Analysis Bulletin.* 7(26) 39-43 in James, M. & Jongeward, D. (1971*). Born to win.*

Reading, PA: Addison-Wesley Publishing Company. 87.

[102] *Ibid.*

[103] Grof, C. (1993). *The thirst for wholeness: Attachment, addiction and the spiritual path.* New York: HarperCollins. 173.

[104] Arrien, A. (1993). *The four-fold way.* San Francisco: HarperCollins. 52.

[105] Steindl-Rast, D. (1984). *Gratefulness, the heart of prayer: An approach to life in fullness.* New York: Paulist Press. 217.

[106] Kripalvanand, S. (1977). *The science of meditation.* Bombay, India: New Karnodaya Press. 164-67.

[107] Kornfield, J. (1991). Vipassana teachers adopt code of ethics. *Turning Wheel.* 27-28.

[108] Butler, K. (Sep/Oct 1990). Spirituality reconsidered: Facing the limits of psychotherapy. *The Family Therapy Networker.* 29.

[109] *Ibid.*

[110] Brown, D. (1994). (Speaker). *Spiritual emergence in the Judeo-Christian tradition.* (Audiotape) Clinical Issues in Psycho Spiritual Crisis. Symposium in Santa Clara, CA: University of California at Santa Cruz.

[111] *Ibid.*

[112] Kripalvanand, S. (1977). *The science of meditation.* Bombay,

India: New Karnodaya Press. 144-156, 196, 199.

[113] Rajneesh, B.S. (1975). *I am the gate: The meaning of initiation and discipleship.* New York: Harper Colophon Books. 56.

[114] The archetypes for this include Shakti reaching for Shiva, the Gopis in divine love with Krishna, and the vows of a Catholic nun as the bride of Christ.

[115] Yogananda, P. (1946). *Autobiography of a yogi.* Los Angeles: Self Realization Fellowship.

Rama, S. (1978). *Living with the himalayan masters.* Honesdale, PA: Himalayan International Institute of Yoga Science & Philosophy.

[116] Grof, C. (1993). *The thirst for wholeness: Attachment, addiction and the spiritual path.* New York: HarperCollins. 230.

[117] Hedges, L. E. (May/June 1993). In praise of the dual relationship: An anthropological insight into how psychotherapy "hooks into the flesh" through dual relationships. *The California therapist.* 46.

[118] Reprinted from *AAMFT Code of Ethics* Copyright August 1991, American Association for Marriage and Family Therapy. Reprinted with permission. No additional copies may be made without obtaining permission from AAMFT.

[119] American Psychological Association. (1992). *Ethical principles of psychologists and code of conduct.* American Psychologist.

[120] National Association for Music Therapy. *Code of Ethics.* 4.5.

[121] *Ethical Guidelines for Feminist Therapists.* Boulder, CO: The Feminist Therapy Institute, Inc.

[122] Manning, R. (1992). *Speaking from the heart: A feminist perspective on ethics.* Lanham, MD: Rowman & Littlefield Publishers, Inc. 98-99.

[123] Fortune, M. M. (1992). *Is nothing sacred?* San Francisco: HarperSanFrancisco. 99-107.

[124] Mindell, A. (1993). *The shaman's body.* San Francisco: HarperSanFrancisco. 167, 191.

[125] Taylor, K. (1994). *The breathwork experience: Exploration and healing in nonordinary states of consciousness.* Santa Cruz, CA: Hanford Mead Publishers. 38.

[126] Hedges, L. E. (Sep/Oct 1993). In praise of the dual relationship: An anthropological insight into how psychotherapy "hooks into the flesh" through dual relationships. *The California therapist.* 38.

[127] *Ibid.*

[128] Ross, C. (1994). *Osiris complex: Case-Studies in multiple personality disorder.* Toronto: University of Toronto Press. 97.

[129] *Ibid.* 77.

[130] Chase, T. (1987). *When rabbit howls.* New York: Jove Books. 62, 85.

[131] Newport, R. R. (1995). *Personal Communication.*

[132] Guggenbühl-Craig, A. (1971, 1982). *Power in the helping professions.* Dallas, TX: Spring Publications, Inc. 28.

[133] Arrien, A. (1993). *The four-fold way.* San Francisco: HarperCollins. 15.

[134] *Ibid.* 82.

[135] *Diagnostic and statistical manual of mental disorders.* Fourth edition. Washington, D.C: American Psychiatric Association. 755-757.

[136] *Ethical Guidelines for Feminist Therapists.* Boulder, CO: The Feminist Therapy Institute, Inc.

[137] Guggenbühl-Craig, A. (1971, 1982). *Power in the helping professions.* Dallas, TX: Spring Publications, Inc. 30.

[138] Williamson, M. (Jan/Feb 1995). In Between heaven and earth. *Common Boundary.* 46.

[139] Guggenbühl-Craig, A. (1971, 1982). *Power in the helping professions.* Dallas, TX: Spring Publications, Inc. 135.

[140] *Ibid.* 148.

[141] Disciplinary actions. (Nov/Dec 1993 through Sept/Oct 1994). *The California therapist.*

[142] Brock, G.W. & Coufal, J. D. (Mar/Apr 1989). Ethics in practice. *The Family Therapy Networker.* 27.

[143] Ethical agreements for Holotropic Breathwork practitioners. (August, 1994). *The Inner Door.* Santa Cruz, CA: Association for Holotropic Breathwork International. 5.

[144] Kornfield, J. (1991). Vipassana teachers adopt code of ethics. *Turning Wheel.* 27-28.

[145] Ziegler, K. (1995). *Personal communication.*

[146] *Ibid.*

[147] Grof, C. (1993). *The thirst for wholeness: Attachment, addiction and the spiritual path.* New York: HarperCollins. 243.

[148] *Ibid.* 237.

[149] *Ibid.*

[150] Rolf Institute. *Code of Ethics.* 5.

[151] *Code of ethics.* (1995). Palo Alto, CA: Jin Shin Do ® Foundation.

[152] Kornfield, J. (1991). Vipassana teachers adopt code of ethics. *Turning Wheel.* 27-28.

[153] *Interim Code of Ethics.* Australia: The N.S.W., Victorian, and Queensland Emotional Release Counsellors Associations.

[154] *Ibid.*

[155] American Group Psychotherapy Association, Inc. (1991). *Guidelines for ethics.* 2.

[156] Reprinted from *AAMFT Code of Ethics* Copyright August 1991, American Association for Marriage and Family Therapy. Reprinted with permission. No additional copies may be made without obtaining permission from AAMFT.

[157] *Interim Code of Ethics.* Australia: The N.S.W., Victorian, and Queensland Emotional Release Counsellors Associations.

[158] Ethical agreements for Holotropic Breathwork practitioners. (August, 1994). *The Inner Door.* Santa Cruz, CA: AHBI. 5.

[159] Rolf Institute. *Code of Ethics.* 2.

[160] Kornfield, J. (1991). Vipassana teachers adopt code of ethics. *Turning Wheel.* 27-28.

[161] Rolf Institute. *Code of Ethics.* 2.

[162] *Code of ethics.* (1995). Palo Alto, CA: Jin Shin Do ® Foundation, and Evergreen, CO: Associated Bodywork and Massage Professionals.

[163] Rolf Institute. *Code of Ethics.* 4.

[164] *Ethical Guidelines for Feminist Therapists.* Denver, CO: The Feminist Therapy Institute, Inc.

[165] Rolf Institute. *Code of Ethics.* 3.

[166] Kornfield, J. (1991). Vipassana teachers adopt code of ethics. *Turning Wheel.* 27-28.

[167] *Code of ethics.* (1995). Palo Alto, CA: Jin Shin Do ® Foundation.

[168] Grof, S. & Grof, C. (1990). Principles of Holotropic Breathwork. In Taylor, K. (1991). *The Holotropic Breathwork workshop:*

A manual for trained facilitators.
79.

[169] Ethical agreements for Holotropic Breathwork practitioners. (August, 1994). *The Inner Door.* Santa Cruz, CA: Association for Holotropic Breathwork International. 5.

[170] *Code of ethics.* (1995). Palo Alto, CA: Jin Shin Do ® Foundation.

[171] Rolf Institute. *Code of Ethics.* 1.

[172] *Principles of medical ethics.* (1993). Washington, D.C.: American Psychiatric Association.

[173] Ethical agreements for Holotropic Breathwork practitioners. (August, 1994). *The Inner Door.* Santa Cruz, CA: Association for Holotropic Breathwork International. 5.

[174] American Association of Professional Hypnotherapists. (1995). *Personal correspondence.*

[175] American Association of Professional Hypnotherapists. *AAPH pledge of professional responsibility.* Boones Mill, VA: AAPH.

[176] *AAAOM oriental medicine ethics statement.* (Draft version-1995). American Association of Acupuncture and Oriental Medicine.

[176] American Psychological Association. (1992). *Ethical principles of psychologists and code of conduct.* American Psychologist.

[177] American Psychological Association. (1992*). Ethical principles*

of psychologists and code of conduct. American Psychologist.

[178] Hedges, L. E. (Sep/Oct 1993). In praise of the dual relationship: An anthropological insight into how psychotherapy "hooks into the flesh" through dual relationships. *The California therapist.* 41.

$\mathcal{S}$elected Bibliography

Achterberg, J. (1985). *Imagery in healing*. Boston: New Science Library. 37-45.

Arrien, A. (1993). *The four-fold way*. San Francisco: HarperCollins.

Bragdon, E. (1990*)*. *The call of spiritual emergency*. San Francisco, CA: Harper & Row, Publishers.

Bragdon, E. (1988). *A sourcebook for helping people in spiritual emergency*. Los Altos, CA: Lightening Up Press.

Brown, D. P. & Fromm, E. (1986). *Hypnotherapy and hypnoanalysis*. Hillsdale, NJ: Lawrence Erlbaum Associates, Publishers.

Campbell, D. (1991). *Music: Physician for times to come*. Wheaton, IL: Quest Books.

Claire, T. (1985). *Bodywork*. New York: William Morrow and Company, Inc.

Eliade, M. (1964). *Shamanism: Archaic techniques of ecstasy*. Princeton, NJ: Princeton University Press.

Fortune, M. M. (1992). *Is nothing sacred?* San Francisco: HarperSanFrancisco. 99-107.

Ingerman, S. (1991). *Soul retrieval: Mending the fragmented self.* San Francisco: HarperCollins.

Grof, C. (1993). *The thirst for wholeness: Attachment, addiction and the spiritual path*. New York: HarperCollins.

Grof, C. & Grof, S. (1990). *The stormy search for the self: A guide to personal growth through transformational crisis.* Los Angeles: Jeremy P. Tarcher, Inc.

Grof, S. & Grof, C. (Eds.) (1989). *Spiritual emergency: When personal transformation becomes a crisis.* Los Angeles: Jeremy Tarcher.

Grof, S. (1988). *The adventure of self-discovery.* Albany, NY: State University of New York Press.

Grof, S. (1985). *Beyond the brain.* Albany, NY: State University of New York Press.

Grof, S. (1980). *LSD Psychotherapy.* Pomona, CA: Hunter House, Inc. Publishers.

Grof, S. (1975). *Realms of the human unconscious: Observations from LSD research.* New York: The Viking Press.

Guggenbühl-Craig, A. (1971, 1982). *Power in the Helping Professions.* Dallas, TX: Spring Publications, Inc.

Herman, J. (1992). *Trauma and recovery.* New York: Basic Books.

Keith-Spiegel, P. & Koocher, G. B. (1985). *Ethics in psychology: Professional standards and cases.* New York: Random House.

Kornfield, J. (1993). *A path with heart: A guide through the perils and promises of spiritual life.* New York: Bantam.

Kornfield, J. (1993). *Teachings of the Buddha.* Boston: Shambhala Publications, Inc.

Mack, J. (1994). *Abductions.* New York: Charles Scribner's Sons.

Manning, R. (1992). *Speaking from the heart: A feminist perspective on ethics.* Lanham, MD: Rowman & Littlefield Publishers, Inc.

Mindell, A. (1993). *The shaman's body.* San Francisco: Harper-SanFrancisco.

Muktananda, S. (1974). *Play of consciousness*. Oakland, CA: S.Y.D.A. Foundation.

Ott, J. (1993). *Pharmacotheon*. Kennewick, WA: Natural Products.

Pope, K. S. & Vasquez, M. J. T. (1991). *Ethics in psychotherapy*. San Francisco: Jossey Bass, Inc. 75.

Pope, K. S. & Bouhoutsos, J. C. (1986). *Sexual intimacy between therapists and patients*. New York: Praeger. 10.

Ring, K. (1984). *Heading toward omega: In search of the meaning of the near-death experience*. New York: William Morrow and Company, Inc.

Ross, C. (1994). *Osiris complex: Case-Studies in multiple personality disorder*. Toronto: University of Toronto Press.

Ross, C. (1989). *Multiple personality disorder*. New York: John Wiley & Sons.

Rutter, P. (1989). *Sex in the forbidden zone*. Los Angeles: Jeremy P. Tarcher.

Sannella, L. (1976). *Kundalini: Psychosis or transcendence?* San Francisco: H.S. Dakin Company.

Schweitzer, A. (1966). *Reverence for life*. New York: Harper & Row Publishers.

Smith, M. (1993). *Ritual abuse*. San Francisco: HarperCollins.

Sparks, T. (1993). *The wide open door: The Twelve Steps, spiritual tradition & the new psychology*. Center City, MN: Hazelden.

Spence, D. P. (1982). *Narrative truth and historical truth: Meaning and interpretation in psychoanalysis*. New York: W.W. Norton & Co., Inc.

Taylor, K. (1994). *The breathwork experience: Exploration and healing in nonordinary states of consciousness*. Santa Cruz, CA: Hanford Mead Publishers.

Wolinsky, S. (1991). *Trances people live: Healing approaches to quantum psychology*. Falls Village, CT: The Bramble Company.

ndex

About the Author

Kylea Taylor is a California Marriage and Family Therapist (MFC# 34901). She worked in the field of addiction recovery and trauma recovery for 30 years and has studied the theory and practice of therapeutic work with clients in non-ordinary states with Christina and Stanislav Grof, M.D., Ph.D. since 1984.

The Ethics of Caring has been published in German by Bauer Verlag under the title of *Helfe für die Helfer*. Kylea Taylor is also the author of *The Breathwork Experience: Exploration and Healing in Nonordinary States of Consciousness* (Hanford Mead, 1994) and numerous articles. She is a Certified Holotropic Breathwork™ Practitioner, a member of the teaching staff of the Grof Transpersonal Training, and has served as editor of *The Inner Door,* the quarterly newsletter of the Association for Holotropic Breathwork International, since 1991.

Other Books from

Hanford Mead Publishers, Inc.

www.hanfordmead.com
www.soulcollage.com
www.ethicsofcaring.com
1.888.727.7310
1.831.459.6855

The
Breathwork
Experience

Exploration and Healing in
Nonordinary States of Consciousness

Kylea Taylor

ISBN #: 0964315807

The Breathwork Experience: Exploration and Healing in Nonordinary States of Consciousness by Kylea Taylor. Soft Cover, 192 pp. $16.95.

A clear, concise, and complete description of breathwork using examples from actual breathwork experiences in participants' own words. Discusses the theories of Stanislav Grof, M.D. and the opportunities in breathwork for healing trauma and assisting recovery from addiction.

www.hanfordmead.com
1.888.727.7310

ISBN #: 096431584X

SoulCollage: An Intuitive Collage Process for Individuals and Groups by Seena B. Frost. Soft Cover, 175 pp. $24.95

The book describes an easy, intuitive collage process. Frost tells how to create a beautiful deck of cards that has deep personal meaning and uses the language of symbols, dreams, and archetypes to answer life's questions. Similar to Tarot, but completely unique to each individual, SoulCollage can be used as a personal spiritual practice or as a satisfying way to encourage identification and expression of inner feelings in other educational, spiritual, or therapeutic group settings. SoulCollage has been used in the Grof Training as an alternative to mandala drawing. The interactive website displays a gallery of cards from the personal decks of others in color.

www.soulcollage.com
1.888.727.7310

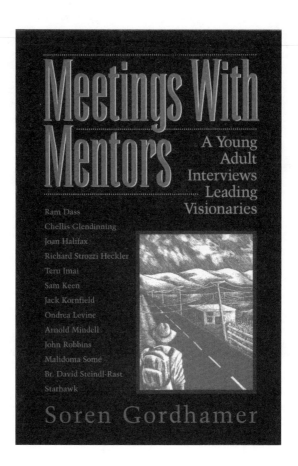

ISBN #: 0964315831

***Meetings with Mentors: A Young Adult Interviews Leading
Visionaries*** by Soren Gordhamer. Soft Cover, 288 pp. $17.95.

A wonderful gift to help someone find his or her own path with
heart. Ram Dass, Jack Kornfield, Joan Halifax, and a dozen other
teachers and authors agreed to tell their personal stories to this
twentysomething author. He asks them about mentorship, rites of
passage, right livelihood, social action, and how to live in a way
that is inwardly rich and outwardly responsible.

www.hanfordmead.com
1.888.727.7310

ISBN # 0894868675

The Wide Open Door: The Twelve Steps, Spiritual Tradition & the New Psychology by Tav Sparks. Soft Cover, 222 pp. $12.00.

This book connects The Twelve Steps of Alcoholics Anonymous to some of the world's greatest spiritual philosophies, Jungian psychology, yoga, the Tao, tribal rites of passage, and more. The book invites us to rediscover the Source behind the Steps through direct personal experience within ourselves and with our Higher Power. The author discusses the experiences of surrender, death and rebirth, and wholeness. He also describes Eleventh Step techniques, such as breathwork — those inner experiences which maintain and deepen recovery.

www.hanfordmead.com
1.888.727.7310

Reviews of *The Ethics of Caring*

This book [*The Ethics of Caring*] is six years old. Why am I reviewing it now? Because, to my chagrin, I only recently discovered it. I wish I'd read it much sooner. Fortunately, it's still easily available on-line, through the publisher at: http://www.hanfordmead.com .

Each one of the "helping professions" has its own professional organization and its own professional code of ethics. There are books written to help counselors and therapists understand these codes and apply them to perplexing situations. Most such books read like legal casebooks. The idea is to help us avoid the consequences of code infractions: professional sanctions or even lawsuits. The code itself is not to be questioned, just applied.

That is certainly important information for professional practitioners who want to keep their licenses and avoid liability suits. But it's not the whole story. We need to think about avoiding harm to clients and ourselves, of course. But it's surely at least as important to think about how to go beyond what is proper or legal to what is best. Taylor's approach does this. She's not satisfied with just avoiding preventable problems. Her goal, instead, is to help her readers create and maintain "right relationship" with their clients. She's also concerned to help practitioners develop an internal locus of control, a strong personal sense of wise, kind and helpful ways to work with people, an ethic of care instead of rules.

Because of this, you won't find dogmatic judgmental statements in this book. Instead, Taylor takes a nuanced and compassionate approach. By understanding how good people become confused about what they should or should not do, we are both warned and strengthened. Her chapters on money, sex and power contain some of the most insightful discussions of these complex issues that I have ever seen.

The book's structure is based on the chakra system. This is the traditional Hindu theory that there are seven energy centers in the body, each related to a different aspect of life. For each chakra, Taylor discusses the focal issues for both helper and client. The writing is mostly clear and accessible, with good endnotes and a glossary.

Taylor's own therapeutic practice, as with many alternative or New Age approaches, involves a lot of work with clients in altered states of consciousness. So the core of the book is an exploration of the special needs, issues and vulnerabilities of people in trance. Any counselor who uses hypnosis, guided fantasy, or similar approaches will find this emphasis particularly helpful.

I certainly hope a second edition will be forthcoming, and soon! If it is, there are some places where some light editing would improve things just a bit. There's a good deal of redundancy in Chapter 2. I would also like to see a franker discussion of co-dependency in Chapter 8. She alludes to these issues, but does not explicitly name the dysfunction she describes.

Quibbles aside, this book is the best of its sort I've seen so far!

Reviewed by Judy Harrow in the
Newsletter for the New Jersey Association for Spiritual, Ethical & Religious Values in Counseling
June 2002

Kylea Taylor's *The Ethics Of Caring* is an extraordinarily helpful and ground-breaking new book for healers, clergy, and therapists that illuminates what is necessary to offer wise and trustworthy relations to their clients. *The Ethics of Caring* alerts healers to not underestimate the power of energies that arise in non-ordinary states through transference and counter-transference, and the palpable physical, emotional, and psychic vulnerabilities that come in these states and provides tools for navigating these deep and often confusing relationship elements. Only by understanding their own vulnerabilities can caregivers hope to enter more fully into truly healing relationships with their clients.

Reviewed by Mid-West Book Review
1996

Kylea Taylor's *The Ethics of Caring*, is in essence about "honoring the web of life in our professional Healing relationships." This work is aimed at a wide audience of healers, doctors, clergy, therapists, and bodyworkers. It centers around developing wisdom and trust in the healer/patient relationship. Kylea grounds her system of ethics in that great philosophical principle known as Reverence for Life. She expands Reverence for Life into a way of knowing/acting in crisis or trauma, loss and grief work, spiritual counseling, expanded consciousness, energetic and shamanic openings. She urges us as healers not to underestimate the energies that arise in non-ordinary states through transference, and countertransference. She also urges us to be aware of and able to deal ethically with the palpable physical, emotional and psychic vulnerabilities that arise in such states. Taylor discusses profound and intense client experiences such as non-ordinary states arising during therapy, the special needs of clients in non-ordinary states of consciousness, a model for examining our vulnerabilities. She discusses money, sex, power, love, truth, insight, and oneness relating each one to a spiritual center. Especially important for the practitioner are Taylor's chapters on vulnerabilities to unethical behavior, and keys to professional ethical behavior.

Reviewed by Brendan Reed, Lac.
in *The Library Letter*, Winter 1996
Bastyr University

I want to highly recommend Kylea's book, *The Ethics of Caring*. It is truly in a class by itself in the literature on ethics in therapy. I've read many books in this area and have been on a Board responsible for reviewing and approving the code of ethics for a large professional association, the American Association for Marriage and Family Therapists (AAMFT), and, to my knowledge, Kylea's book is unique in the field. It combines the rigors of professionalism with a deep and complex understanding of the human heart, soul and mind. It really is an important book. If you are a professor or teacher you might want to consider it as required reading.

Reviewed by Sara Wright, Ph.D.
Licensed Psychologist
Licensed Marriage & Family Therapist
Board Member, American Association for Marriage and Family Therapy (AAMFT)
Past-President, Minnesota Association for Marriage and Family Therapy (MAMFT)
July 2002